Pyles, Mary.
    Everyday cat : the complete guide to
understanding and enjoying your pet cat /
Mary Pyles ; photos by Larry Johnson and
James Curtis ; illustrated by Sidney Giffin
Wiley. -- New York : Howell Book House,
c1991.

    207 p. : ill.   **25346**

    ISBN 0-87605-840-3(lib. bdg.) : $20.00

                                    MAR '93

    1. Cats.   I. Title.

                                    14
                            WLF00-440880
                                    MARC

EVERYDAY
CAT

EVERYDAY
CAT

*The Complete Guide to Understanding
and Enjoying Your Pet Cat*

Mary Pyles

Photos by Larry Johnson
and James Curtis

Illustrated by Sidney Giffin Wiley

HOWELL
BOOK HOUSE

New York

Maxwell Macmillan Canada
TORONTO

Maxwell Macmillan International
NEW YORK   OXFORD   SINGAPORE   SYDNEY

Copyright © 1991 by Mary Pyles

Howell Book House
Macmillan Publishing Company
866 Third Avenue
New York, NY 10022

Maxwell Macmillan Canada, Inc.
1200 Eglinton Avenue East, Suite 200
Don Mills, Ontario M3C 3N1

Macmillan Publishing Company is part of the Maxwell Communication Group of Companies.

Library of Congress Cataloging-in-Publication Data

Pyles, Mary.
    Everyday cat : the complete guide to understanding and enjoying
  your pet cat / by Mary Pyles.
      p.   cm.
    ISBN 0-87605-840-3
    1. Cats. I. Title.
  SF442.P94   1991   90-35470
  363.8 — dc20

Macmillan books are available at special discounts for bulk purchases for sales promotions, premiums, fund-raising, or educational use. For details contact:

                Special Sales Director
                Macmillan Publishing Company
                866 Third Avenue
                New York, NY 10022

10 9 8 7 6 5 4 3 2 1

Printed in the United States of America

*This book is lovingly dedicated
to Ming, Miep, Malachi, Mishia,
Shadwick, Shalimar and Sabrina,
the Hope Haven rescues*

Contents

Preface

This book evolved from my work in cat rescue and deep concern over the large numbers of healthy cats destroyed in shelters every year. It troubles me that many cats are adopted only to be returned to a shelter simply because a potential owner does not have the knowledge to deal successfully with a secondhand cat and the problems it sometimes has. Healthy cats, returned with claims that they are mean-tempered, are often euthanized needlessly. Usually the problem is a frightened cat, not a mean cat.

One of the factors contributing to the crowded conditions at our shelters is the volume of returnees. Unfortunately, many cats are returned because they do not immediately live up to an adopter's expectations. I hope that, with the knowledge of how to work with the secondhand or rescued cat that you will learn in this book, the number of returnees can be noticeably reduced.

One of the greatest animal-related problems we face in the United States today is the overpopulation of cats. Thousands of lovely cats are put down every year because of overcrowding at shelters and lack of homes.

A major cause of overcrowding is the failure of cat owners to spay or neuter. Many intact cats are allowed to roam freely, populating the world with vast numbers of unwanted kittens.

In recent years the increase in the popularity of the cat has created more backyard breeders and kitten mills. These people breed indiscriminately in a quest for quick profits. The offspring of such matings are generally poor examples of a particular breed, and many of these cats also end their days in our overworked shelters.

The purpose of this book is to give the cat owner a more complete understanding of the companion cat and to promote responsible cat ownership by encouraging spay/neutering along with giving of quality care in order that the household pet cat can reach its full potential.

Acknowledgments

A warm special thanks to Sidney Wiley for her beautiful illustrations. Her support and encouragement were there from the moment of this book's inception. To work with her is a joy.

To Kay and Mary Ann, two very special dedicated cat rescuers, thank you for encouraging me to write this book.

I have received a great deal of help from Dorothy Lewis and the Happy Household Pet Cat Club. My deep appreciation to all my fellow members for your help and pictures.

My thanks and gratitude to Seymour Weiss, my editor, who believed in me and this project.

EVERYDAY
CAT

1

Choosing Your Cat

T HE POPULARITY OF THE CAT as a companion animal has grown steadily in recent years. Cat lovers attribute this to the unique personality, independent spirit and beauty of the domestic feline. The tremendous capacity for adaptability and apparent self-sufficiency are some of the reasons claimed by others in trying to explain the popularity phenomenon of the cat.

The advantages of the cat as a house pet are numerous. The average purchase price of a purebred cat is well within reach of most prospective owners. Undocumented purebreds and mixed-bred cats may be adopted for little or no money. The maintenance costs of a cat are significantly lower than comparable amounts for the canine companion.

The cat is known for being a scrupulously clean animal both in its personal hygiene habits and living areas. It generally will adapt to a litter pan with little or no training, thereby eliminating the need for its owner to be home to walk it several times a day.

The cat demands less attention and care than some other types of pets. This animal adapts perfectly to living an indoor life, while a dog must have a certain amount of daily outdoor exercise. The cat can be equally happily confined to a small, urban apartment or having the run of a large, suburban house and yard.

The cat provides humans with companionship, love and loyalty, even though the cat's love must be earned. When given, that love is lifelong and can survive even a prolonged separation from its human. The cat gives affection without making too many demands.

Morris the 9-Lives Cat lends a paw during Adopt-a-Cat Month. © 1990 Heinz Pet Products Co., owner of the registered trademark Morris the 9-Lives Cat. Used with permission.

There are some responsibilities to owning any animal. Shelters and pounds are filled with large numbers of unwanted pets because the novelty of owning a playful kitten or the status of having a particular breed has worn thin. Before choosing a cat, there are a number of questions you should ask yourself.

Are you going to go into a frenzy when that cute cat breaks your favorite lamp while performing his morning calisthenics? Will you become annoyed when that fabulous feline eats part of a houseplant, then throws up on your bedspread? Can you cope with finding cat hair in your coffee and on your clothes? If these minor annoyances are enough to send you screaming, then think about choosing fish. If you feel that you can cope calmly with the occasional disturbance, then chances are that you and a cat can live in harmony and happiness.

To have a relationship with your cat that is mutually satisfying, you have to do more than just feed it and change the litter box. Every cat depends on a daily play-and-chat session with you. If you live alone and spend a great deal of time away from home, then seriously consider acquiring two cats. This way the cats will be company for each other and will not be deprived of companionship.

ADULT OR KITTEN?

In deciding whether to select a kitten or adult, ask yourself how much time you will have to spend training and raising the animal. Is the age of the cat an important issue to you? Are there young children in your home who could easily hurt a small kitten?

Kittens require a great deal of time and attention for the first few months of life. A kitten will try to get into everything, never learning to respect your possessions unless you take the time to teach it the socially acceptable behavior of your home. You could well have the responsibility of training the kitten to use the litter pan.

For an elderly person or the busy pet owner, it is best to select an adult cat. Chances are the adult cat will already have been litter trained. The adult is more sober in its ways and therefore beyond that mischievous kitten stage of wanting to play with everything in sight. The adult cat may well have been taught good manners by its previous owner.

Unless you are purchasing a purebred cat and are familiar with the personality traits of that breed, the personality of the kitten may well come as a surprise when it reaches adulthood. Not all breeds have the same personality traits as adults.

The personality of the adult cat is readily apparent. You can tell whether it is an affectionate lap cat or a standoffish independent animal that will share your home but not your bed. Any undesirable traits or physical or psychological problems are readily ascertained in the mature cat.

At first a kitten may feel the loss of its littermates and mother, but it will get over this longing rapidly and integrate into a new family life rather quickly.

3

Two cats in a household will provide companionship for each other.

The impish kitten likes to play with anything in its sight. *James Curtis*

A kitten can provide you with endless hours of entertainment as you watch it grow from playful imp into a lovely, mature adult.

The adult cat often takes a great deal longer to adjust to a new home. If the adult had established a long, close loving relationship with a previous owner, it may be months before it is emotionally secure with a new owner.

MALE OR FEMALE?

For a responsible pet owner who does not intend to breed, it makes little difference whether you select a male or female. Both are equally intelligent and affectionate. A male may be slightly bigger, while the female generally is daintier in appearance. The real difference in selecting the sex of your pet is whether or not you have the animal spayed or neutered.

A tom or whole male is more aggressive than the neutered male. Male kittens begin to sexually mature at around eight months. If allowed outside, he will roam the neighborhood looking for a mate. This leads to unwanted litters of kittens and cat fights with other stud males. The whole male will begin to spray indoors to mark his territories. The odor of this spray is very unpleasant, and it is difficult to remove from carpet and drapes.

A female kitten that is left unspayed generally is easier to keep than the whole male. She does not tend to spray like the tom, but keep in mind that some females will spray. The female may start to call as early as six months. After that she can come into heat as often as every three weeks during the breeding season. If she has access to a tom, then you will have an unwanted litter.

LONG-HAIRED OR SHORT-HAIRED?

In selecting a cat, it is important to consider this question very seriously. If you are a busy person with very little time to devote to grooming your cat, then a short-haired cat is probably the best for you. The occasional combing and brushing is all that is basically necessary with a short-haired breed.

Long-haired breeds, while beautiful, do demand a great deal of time to keep the coat looking its best. Daily combing is necessary to keep the long coat free of mats and tangles. If the long-haired cat is allowed outside, then weekly baths are a must.

RANDOM BRED OR PUREBRED

This is a matter of individual preference. The cat of unknown parentage makes just as warm and loving a companion as does the cat that comes from a line of many grand champions. Remember, it's not the cat who cares about ancestry, it's the human who places importance on pedigrees. In the United

Long-haired cats are beautiful but require a great deal of time and care. *Larry Johnson*

States more than 90 percent of the household pet cats are ordinary cats without fancy pedigrees.

The breeding of purebred cats is a recent phenomenon. There are physical and temperamental differences between the various breeds. If you are attracted by a particular breed, then a purebred animal is probably best for you. In theory, a purebred cat should be more free from hereditary defects and have more predictable character traits than the random-bred cat, but this is not necessarily true in practice.

If the pedigree is not important to you, then there is nothing wrong with the random-bred cat. I live with both and have found there is no difference. The common, ordinary random-bred cat is as healthy, playful and active as its pure-bred cousin.

FINDING A CAT

Should you want a purebred cat, your first priority is to select a breed. If you are undecided about exactly what breed you would like, then take time to visit a local cat show. There you will have the opportunity to see examples of most breeds. Talk to breeders and ask them questions about the advantages and disadvantages of their particular breed. There are a number of good books available at your local library that explain all the different breeds.

The best way to buy a purebred cat is directly from a reputable breeder. For a nominal fee the Cat Fanciers' Association will send you a directory of the more than three thousand registered CFA breeders in the United States. Whether you purchase a purebred cat locally or from an out-of-town breeder, check the reputation of the breeder first. You can do this by calling the cat registry the breeder uses, a local cat club or Better Business Bureau in the breeder's area or with breeders of the same breed in your area.

A purebred cat is not inexpensive. The better the quality, the higher the price will be. The price of this cat will cover the breeder's expenses of caring for the queen, the stud fee and care, feeding and inoculations of the kittens after birth.

Generally speaking, a nice random-bred cat can be found at little or no cost. Due to the fact that thousands of unwanted litters are born every year, ads for "free-to-good-home" and low-cost kittens can be found in abundance in the classified section of most newspapers. Usually this is a case of where the neighbor's male paid a visit to the female next door or someone thought it would be nice to breed their female just once in order to experience the so-called joys of the birth of kittens. Now they have found this joy was a myth, and the owner is desperate to find good homes for the litter.

Many nice cats with parentage unknown can be found in animal shelters. Usually a shelter charges a nominal sum to cover the cost of inoculations and spay/neutering. As thousands of cats are destroyed monthly in the United States, these shelters try to make adoption as easy and inexpensive as possible in order

Waiting for her owner, this lovely random-bred seems unconcerned about pedigrees. *JamesCurtis*

This fortunate random-bred was saved by adoption to a good home. *James Curtis*

to save animals whenever possible. Most shelters have a policy of only putting animals that appear to be healthy up for adoption.

Morris, the 9-Lives cat, was a typical example of a shelter cat. Bob Martwick, on behalf of 9-Lives, found Morris in a New England animal shelter. Since that day, this random-bred cat has become a national celebrity. He was the spokescat for the 9-Lives food products and starred in their television commercials.

The Morris character has come a long way since then. It is the spokescat for a month-long adopt-a-cat program sponsored by 9-Lives and the American Humane Association. For more than fifteen years, Morris has worked with animal shelters across the country to promote the adoption of cats as companion animals. He aids in the educational program of responsible pet ownership.

Approximately 15 million healthy cats are dumped in animal shelters every year. About 80 percent of these cats die by euthanasia because homes cannot be found for them. Most of our shelters are so overcrowded that healthy cats are destroyed within three to five days after arrival.

June is national adopt-a-cat month. It has been one of history's longest-running pet projects. The program is credited with placing over a million cats in pet homes.

Last but definitely not least is the stray. These cats can be found almost anywhere. Oftentimes they will try to adopt you. You may find one turning up on your doorstep or encounter one while shopping or out for a walk. If the cat seems well fed and extremely tame, chances are it lives nearby and is out for its stroll. A thin, ragged cat is generally a stray needing a good home. Unless you have made thorough inquiries about where it belongs, do not take such a cat, as you are in all probability stealing someone's pet. If you do decide to keep a stray, then make an effort to find its owner by placing an ad in your local newspaper and checking with the local shelter for a lost cat. Many shelters have a lost-and-found network.

SELECTING A HEALTHY KITTEN

In selecting a healthy kitten, it is most important to see both the mother and its littermates in their home surroundings. You can deduce a great deal about the health of a potential pet from the conditions in which a litter is kept.

Kittens should be at least six weeks old, and preferably ten to twelve weeks old, before leaving their mother. In choosing a kitten under twelve weeks, it is essential to make sure the animal has been totally weaned from its mother. If you are purchasing a purebred kitten, you will find that a responsible breeder will not consider letting a kitten leave until it is at least three months old. If you should purchase one before this time, most breeders will allow you to visit your kitten during the waiting period so you may get acquainted with it and watch it develop. Most breed registries stipulate that a registered kitten may not be separated from its mother before it is at least twelve weeks old.

Many shelters allow kittens to be adopted at eight weeks because space is

Morris the 9-Lives Cat takes an extra step for his homeless friends during national Adopt-a-Cat Month. © 1990 Heinz Pet Products Co., owner of the registered trademark Morris the 9-Lives Cat. Used with permission.

generally at a premium. Often too, kittens from an unwanted litter are given away around six to eight weeks of age. Circumstance may make it impossible for someone to keep a litter much longer.

Look to see if the surroundings are clean and warm. There should be ample room for the mother to move about and the kittens to play. Overcrowding, dirt and cold temperatures are conditions that are very conducive to disease. Does the area provide for plenty of human contact? Kittens need to have the opportunity for human contact and handling to become good pets.

Healthy kittens are by nature very playful and alert. When viewing a litter, note whether they are playful, wrestle with their siblings and seem alert to each other or their surroundings. The kitten sitting woefully alone in the corner not playing is probably sick, not shy.

Carefully check for signs of ill health. It is important to pick the kitten up and examine the eyes, ears, nose, mouth, coat and hindquarters. Look for signs of diarrhea or loose stool in the litter tray. Pay close attention to the condition of the mother, especially her eyes and nose.

Note the eyes of the kittens to see if they are clear and bright, without a trace of tearing or other discharge. Runny, red or dull eyes are a sign of disease. Protrusion of the third eyelid is a symptom of sickness. Check to see if the nose is cool and dry. A runny nose may indicate a respiratory infection. Look inside the mouth. Healthy gums are pale pink, and the teeth should be white in a kitten, although teeth may be slightly yellow from tartar in an adult. There should be no signs of abnormal redness or inflammation in the mouth. The ears should be examined for excess wax or infection. A kitten that has dark brown, grainy wax inside the ears or is constantly shaking its head and scratching its ears may have ear mites.

The coat should be clean, glossy and free of mats, with no traces of fleas or other parasites. Beware of bald patches, skin sores, dandruff or scales, as this could indicate ringworm and other problems. Turn the kitten over to see the abdomen. It should be full. A potbelly is a sign of roundworms. Feel for any lump that could mean an umbilical hernia. The anus and sex organs should be clean. Observe for any discharge or worms. Diarrhea leaves dirt traces on the coat in this area.

Inquire about the medical background of both the mother and kittens. Ask if the mother has been vaccinated and when. Don't be afraid to ask to see her vaccination certificate. Check to see if the kittens were wormed, along with when and if they have been vaccinated. Be sure to keep this information to give to your veterinarian for his records.

HEALTH OF THE STRAY

Stray cats certainly do not come equipped with any health guarantees and should be taken to a veterinarian before you bring one home, if possible. These cats make wonderful companions, but they often need some type of medical

A stray looking for a home.   *James Curtis*

An example of a healthy kitten.   *Larry Johnson*

attention in the beginning. There is a chance the animal could have ear mites or worms or be suffering from malnutrition.

While you may have an initial outlay the first day to treat for a medical problem, these animals will return your cost a thousandfold with the love they will give you over the years. If the stray is injured and you are willing to provide it with treatment, you will reap the joys of the gratitude and devotion of that cat for many years to come. There is a very special bond that forms between an owner and a cat when you have rescued it and nursed it back to health.

2

Caring for Your Cat

NOW THAT you have acquired a cat, there are a few rules of general care that contribute greatly to the overall well-being of your new pet. Even though the cat is fairly self-sufficient, there are certain things it depends on its human companions to provide for its comfort and health.

INTRODUCING THE NEW HOME

Plan on collecting a new cat at a time when you can give it as much attention as possible. A weekend or holiday is best. For both safety and comfort the cat should be transported in a carrier. This can be purchased reasonably in most pet shops, discount stores or department stores. Line the bottom with a soft cloth. If you are traveling a long distance, it is best not to feed the cat before you start for home.

After reaching home, close all the doors and windows before opening the carrier. The cat is going to be bewildered at first by strange surroundings. Put the carrier in the room that contains its litter pan and shut the door. Lift the cat from the carrier and place it in the litter pan. Let the cat explore this room first so that it will learn where its toilet is kept.

Once the cat has calmed down, allow it to explore the rest of its new home. The cat will slowly begin sniffing and exploring every room. Follow along with it and gently reassure it by talking to it in a soft voice. Kittens are best confined

A bed can be plain or fancy, as long as the cat has enough room and privacy.   *James Curtis*

Cat trees provide a place to climb and sharpen their claws.   *James Curtis*

to one room for a few days until they have gained confidence. Once the cat begins to groom itself, then you will know it is settling in comfortably. This is a good time to offer it food and water.

After the first round of exploration, show the cat where its bed is located. Cats spend a great deal of their time sleeping and tend to please themselves about where they sleep. The bed should be big enough for your cat to stretch out in and be enclosed on at least three sides. This gives the cat a sense of security. Line the bed with some type of soft material, but do not be surprised if the new bed is rejected in favor of your bed at night. A kitten will want to play, but knowing where its bed is located is reassuring. Change the bedding regularly to keep it clean and dry.

Cats like cave-type beds that can serve as a playhouse or hiding place. These can be bought or made. A cardboard box with an opening can be used. Glue the sides and top shut, then cut a round opening on one side about eight inches in diameter. The floor can be padded with a piece of carpet remnant. The advantage to this type is that it can be thrown out and easily replaced when it is soiled.

If you decide to allow your cat to go outdoors, it must feel at home inside before it is allowed the freedom to run outside. Let it explore the new world outside bit by bit. Leave the door open. If the cat becomes frightened, it will dash back to the safety of its home. An intelligent cat can be taught to stay in its own backyard or the immediate vicinity.

Some indoor cats adapt to walking on a leash. For this you will need a harness. I do not recommend this for an outdoor cat. It is too easy for a cat to become startled or spooked. When this happens the cat can wiggle out of the harness and make a frantic rush for a place to hide. It is too easy for the panic-stricken cat to dash in the street and be hit by a car.

A litter tray should be provided and in place before you bring the new cat home. Fill the bottom with about one to one and a half inches of clay litter. It is more economical to purchase litter in twenty-five- or fifty-pound sacks. Plastic litter liners aid in reducing odor.

There is no need to replace the litter every day if the solid wastes are scooped out and disposed of. The pan should be washed once a week with hot soapy water. Strong disinfectants are not recommended because cats do not like the smell and they will look for another place to urinate. A mothball cake hanging in the room with the litter tray will help eliminate odors.

Cat Comforts

A cat has a natural need to sharpen its claws. To protect your furniture, offer it a tempting alternative such as a rug or post for this purpose. A cat tree is ideal for the indoor cat. If you decide to build one yourself, make sure that it is properly balanced and stable. These trees are usually covered with carpet, and a cat will use it for climbing and sharpening claws.

There is a whole array of manufactured cat toys for sale; many have catnip

Cat toys can be purchased or made.   *James Curtis*

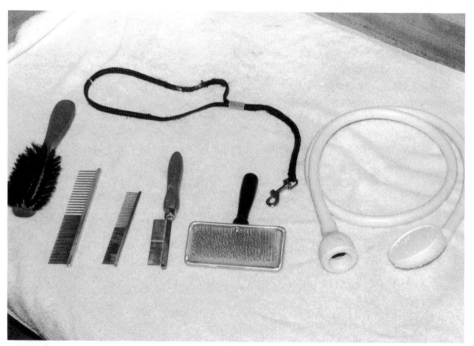

Grooming tools, left to right; natural bristle brush, large-tooth steel comb, small cheek comb, flea comb, slicker brush, noose, spray attachment.   *James Curtis*

inside. Cats also like to play with crumpled balls of foil, soda straws, or Ping-Pong balls. Cat toys can be made from cloth scraps that have been cut into shapes, then filled with pillow stuffing. Paper bags and baskets are also very popular playthings with cats.

Destructive behavior is generally due to boredom. Provide entertainment and exercise for your cat. A collection of strong cardboard boxes and tubes gives the cat endless hours of fun and exercise.

When leaving your cat for any length of time, it is important that your home is safe and comfortable. Cats are tempted by plants. Since many are poisonous, place them out of reach before leaving. Grass grown in a pot provides the greenery a cat needs and may be purchased at a pet store. Leave windows partially open for ventilation if you don't have a central heat and air unit. Apartment owners should not allow the cat access to a balcony unless it is cat-proofed. A balcony can be fitted with a hinged frame covered with wire mesh to form a sun porch. Make sure your home is not too stuffy, drafty or hot for the cat.

GROOMING THE CAT

A sleek, glossy coat reflects the general well-being and health of a cat. Most cats do an excellent job of keeping themselves clean. Supplementing the cat's grooming plays an important role in keeping the animal free of parasites and tangles. Inconsistent grooming is the most common reason for mats and tangles in a long-haired cat. Regular grooming attention by the owner removes loose hair and dandruff along with keeping the eyes and ears clean, and it is an excellent means of spotting potential health problems in the early stages.

It is wise to accustom your cat to daily grooming of its coat from the first day you bring it home. The grooming period can become an enjoyable play period for both you and the cat in addition to a sensible means of keeping the cat clean.

A careful inspection should be made of the skin, watching for parasites and skin disorders. This is important if the cat has come in contact with other cats, perhaps at a cat show or boarding kennel.

The Coat

The most efficient way of finding fleas is combing through the coat with a flea comb. This is a very fine-toothed metal comb with the teeth close together that pick up dead hairs and trap fleas. Start combing on top of the head and work toward the tail. Use small short strokes, combing each area several times before moving on to the next. Be sure to comb the entire cat. After a few strokes, check the comb for fleas. Act quickly to kill them, for fleas are remarkably agile. A glass of hot water is useful for dipping the comb, drowning the live flea.

Before using a flea comb on a long-haired cat, you must use a wide-toothed

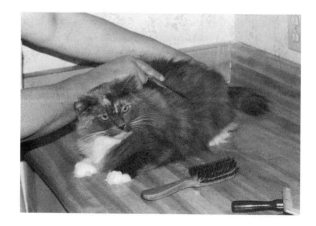

Regular grooming with the large comb removes loose hair and mats in the long-haired cat. *James Curtis*

Use the flea comb to remove parasites.
James Curtis

A good hairball preparation aids in eliminating hair from the digestive tract and intestines.
James Curtis

metal comb to remove tangles. A long-haired cat that is groomed every day should remain free of mats. A coat with fine hair mats and tangles easier than a course-textured coat. Mats are usually found on the belly and between the legs. To remove mats, first gently loosen and separate the tangle with your fingers, then slowly tease it out with the wide-toothed comb. Bad tangles or mats must be carefully cut out with scissors. Once the coat is free of mats, you can use the flea comb.

A hair shaft is composed of three separate layers. The cuticle is the outer layer and its function is to protect the inner layers of hair. The ends of the overlapping scales of the cuticle protrude upward and outward, similar to barbs, in the direction of hair growth. The ragged edges of these barbs lock together to form tangles when there is a lack of oil in the coat. Too much oil causes the hair to become gummy and mat.

The ends of the hair are rather sparse when the kitten coat undergoes the change to an adult coat. The hair at the skin is much thicker. Regular brushing is necessary as the fine kitten hair is being replaced by the coarser adult hair in the same follicle. In a long-haired coat, large and painful mats form almost overnight near the skin. When this happens, it is better to have the coat clipped down. Most cats will not tolerate the time and effort required to remove these tangles from their coats.

During the spring and autumn, cats shed their old coats. Grooming at these times helps prevent hairballs from developing, since cats swallow large amounts of this loose hair when licking. Several good preparations available for elimination and prevention of hairballs are readily available. These are usually an emulsion of liquid petrolatum, glycerine and flavoring and are administered orally.

After combing, brush the coat with a brush made of natural bristle. This type of brush causes less static electricity and broken hairs than synthetic types. The coat can be given a final polish with a piece of soft nylon, silk or chamois.

A greasy coat can be treated with talcum powder or cornstarch to remove the grease. Shake the powder on the coat and gently rub it thoroughly into the hair. Then brush the powder out of the coat. Tar, paint and grease can be removed with a household detergent. In cases of heavy contamination, the coat should be soaked in cooking oil to loosen these substances before bathing. If you think the cat has licked the substance, then consult your veterinarian, as the substance may be poisonous.

Ears, Eyes, Mouth and Claws

During the grooming session, note if the eyes are clear and bright. Any discharge is a sign of a sick cat, and your veterinarian should be consulted. White cats, Persians or cats with a Persian background may have some tear staining around the eyes. This is normal and can be removed with a damp cotton ball or towel.

Check the ears for dirt and mites. Any sign of dirt or wax should be

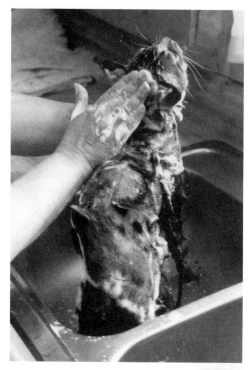

Work the shampoo through the hair into the skin. *James Curtis*

Rinse the cat for as long as it takes to remove any trace of shampoo.
James Curtis

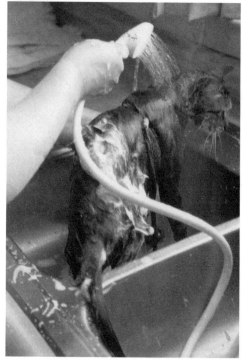

swabbed out with a cotton bud. Moisten a cotton swab with baby oil and remove the excess wax or dirt from the inside of the flap. Never probe down into the ear canal without instructions from your veterinarian. Probing too deep can be dangerous. Normal ear wax is a light honey color. Dark-colored wax may be the first sign of an ear mite infestation, which requires medical attention.

Examine the teeth and gums for any sign of tartar, broken teeth, bad breath, soreness or other disorders. A heavy tartar buildup has to be removed under a light anesthetic. The teeth can be cleaned by gently rubbing with a light application of baking soda or salt on a cotton ball.

The first few times you trim the claws it is best done with the help of another person. Most cats resent this at first. If you do not have help, then wrap the cat securely in a bath towel. You can use special pet clippers available from a pet store or the type used for manicuring humans. Once a week, check the claws to see if they need trimming.

To trim the claws, squeeze the toe between your forefinger and thumb. The claw can easily be extended. Trim the claw, being extremely careful to avoid the sensitive pink quick. Remove only the clear tip.

BATHING A CAT

As a general rule, only bathe a cat when it is dirty or the treatment of a disease requires bathing. A cat washes its coat more than twenty times a day and is capable of keeping it clean. Show cats need more frequent baths.

Bathe the cat in a warm room, and avoid frightening it by running water on it directly from the faucet. A small hose with a spray attachment that fits on the faucet of your sink is one of the best methods for wetting a cat. A rubber mat or thick bath towel placed in the bottom of the sink or bowl will give the cat good footing. A small dab of petroleum jelly around the eyes aids in keeping soap from irritating them.

Using lukewarm water, wet the cat thoroughly. Long hair sheds water, so it takes longer to get this type of coat wet to the skin. When the coat is wet, gradually work in the shampoo. Start with the head and neck, working down to the tail. Work the shampoo through the hair down into the skin. A washcloth can be used to clean the face.

Rinse thoroughly for as long as necessary to remove any trace of the shampoo. A final rinse of vinegar and water may be used. Mix one part vinegar with twelve parts water, then pour through the coat. Rinse again with clear water.

SHOW BATHS

A cat must be immaculately clean when taken to a show. For a show bath, additional shampooing with a coat enhancer or lightener shampoo is helpful. There are several excellent whiteners for light-colored cats. For dark coats, use a specially designed color-enhancer shampoo.

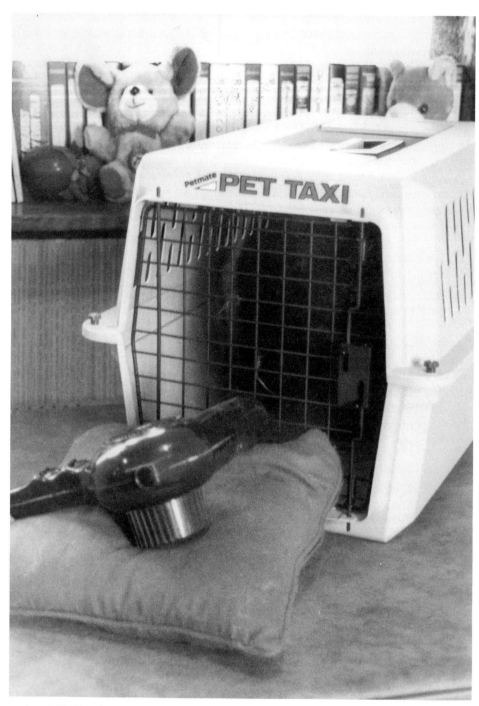

A portable blow dryer and carrier can be used as an inexpensive drying cage. *James Curtis*

You should begin experimenting with shampoos and cream rinses beforehand in order to learn which brands are the best for your cat. You will need to determine how many days after bathing your cat looks its best. Once you have decided this, then you may govern your pre-show bath accordingly. What works for one cat may not work for another.

The first step is to remove any excess grease from the coat. This is done in two parts, using a dish soap such as Dawn or Joy. During the first soaping, pay particular attention to the areas under the front legs, the chest, the top of the base of the tail and the ruff along the back legs. Rinse with a vinegar rinse and wash again in the dish soap. The final rinse is done with clear water.

Now it is time for the coat enhancer. Some products recommend leaving the lather on for a period of five minutes, so make sure you read the label carefully. Rinse with clear water. After this stage you may want to use a cream rinse.

After the final rinse, gently squeeze the excess water from the coat. Pay particular attention to the feet, legs and tail. Wrap the cat in a warm towel and rub its face. Finish drying the cat by placing it in a cage or carrier and use a hair dryer on medium to low heat. Face the dryer toward the cage, on the outside, and let the cat blow dry. In long-haired coats, this method helps reduce tangles and mats. The first time the dryer is turned on the cat might become frightened, but if you stay where the cat can see you and talk to it gently, it will calm down very quickly.

When the cat is partially dry, brush the coat, using long strokes backbrushing against the coat. To achieve a fluffy look with a longhair when the cat is almost dry, remove it from the drying cage. Back-brush the coat while blowing with the dryer until the coat is thoroughly dry. This aerates the coat to give it a full, fluffy look. A shorthair just needs smoothing with the brush and a polish with a soft cloth to look its best.

A cat is fastidious by nature and will generally enjoy its grooming session with you. This can be a pleasurable experience for both you and the cat by using it as a time to play with, cuddle and love your special friend.

TRAVELING WITH THE CAT

Most cats do not take too kindly to traveling. However there will be times when it is necessary to transport your cat, such as for trips to the veterinarian or moving to a new home. On other occasions, when travel is a matter of choice it is best to consider the temperament and age of your cat along with the distance it has to travel before deciding to subject it to what is an uncomfortable and possibly traumatic experience.

When traveling out of town with the cat, make the proper preparations ahead of time. If you are using public transportation, find out their regulations well in advance. It is wise to check hotel policy when making reservations, as many hotels do not accept pets.

Provide a secure carrier when traveling with a cat.

James Curtis

Car and Rail Travel

When traveling by car, always secure a cat safely in a sturdy carrier. Attach the cat's name and address to a collar in case of escape. It is dangerous to allow a cat to roam in a moving car. A cat may become upset and interfere with the driver, causing an accident, or lunge from an open window. The chances of its survival after jumping from a moving vehicle would be slim. Position the carrier so that sudden braking or turning will not upset or throw it on the floor, or secure a seat belt around it. Never store a cat in the trunk of a car.

Never leave a cat unattended in a parked car. This invites theft, and there is a risk of escape. On a hot day it is very easy for the cat to suffer from a heat stroke in a parked vehicle. In cold weather there is a danger of it becoming chilled.

When traveling a long distance, provide the cat with water every four to six hours and the opportunity to use the litter pan. It is best to withhold food immediately before traveling. Cats can suffer from motion sickness. A mild tranquilizer may be prescribed by your veterinarian for a nervous or high-strung cat. When arriving at your destination, keep the carsick or nervous cat quiet with access to water and its litter pan. Cats recover from motion sickness rapidly when left alone and quiet.

Buses and trains accept cats only in approved secure containers. Some trains require that the cat travel in a carrier in the baggage car. If this is the case, then visit the cat frequently and provide it with water. If the cat is traveling unaccompanied by rail, make adequate arrangements for the cat to be collected at its destination. If the journey is longer than twenty-four hours, find out what provisions are made for food and water.

Air and Sea Travel

Each airline has its own regulations regarding the transporting or shipping of live cargo. These regulations are often due to government regulations. Charges will vary between airlines. Cats may only be carried on board an aircraft in an approved carrier. These can often be purchased from the airline, and they can be stowed under the seat. Some airlines require that live animals travel only in the pressurized heated sections in the cargo hold. Make advanced arrangements when traveling by air.

Most airlines will not carry young kittens. It is unwise to ship a pregnant female by air. Only mild tranquilizers should be given and only under veterinarian supervision.

Once airborne, there is no access to the cargo bay. If the cat is in transit for longer than twenty-four hours, you will be required to provide food, along with written feeding instructions. Dry or semimoist is the most convenient. Few airports have boarding facilities, so it is important to make arrangements for the cat to be met by a private individual at its destination.

Most ship accommodations are inadequate for animals. If traveling by ship, you will be allowed to visit the cat frequently. If the cat should become ill, the ship's physician may be able to help you. Seasickness is common in cats, so check with your veterinarian before departure.

Foreign Travel

Before traveling to another country, it is essential that you find out what documentation and vaccinations are required. In most cases you will need a health certificate issued by a licensed veterinarian and within a certain number of days prior to entry into that country. Some countries have a quarantine law for animals, regardless of health or vaccinations. This period varies from one to six months in some countries. Great Britain has a six-month quarantine and the state of Hawaii has a four-month quarantine because they are among the few places that are free of rabies. Check with the embassy or consulate concerned.

If you are traveling to a country where a quarantine is imposed, you generally must make arrangements well in advance with an official kennel facility. In some cases a licensed agent must transfer the cat to the quarantine facility. Cats are required to be vaccinated twice at the owner's expense while in quarantine in Britain. Visits to these quarantine quarters are strictly regulated.

BOARDING A CAT

At some time you will face the problem of what to do with your cat while you are away from home. The ideal arrangement is to have someone look after the cat in its own home, but this is not always possible or practical. The alternative is a boarding establishment. Most establishments accommodate both cats and dogs.

It is wise to make arrangements far in advance of your departure date, if possible. Good boarding facilities are heavily booked during the summer months. Some states have little if any restrictions on kennels; therefore, the standards are left up to the individual operator. Before leaving your cat at one of these places, you would be wise to visit and inspect the facility.

Ask how often the cats are fed and what they are fed. Find out if they are groomed. Check the current boarders if possible to see how well cared for they are and how content they seem to be, along with the cleanliness of their cages. Inquire about isolation quarters. Sick animals should be some distance away from the rest of the boarders. Cats in isolation units should be barrier-nursed. Beware of an establishment that does not require proof of up-to-date vaccinations and a health certificate.

Many facilities will allow cats from the same household to be housed together, if you desire. Never allow your cats to share the same accommodation with cats from a different household.

Many veterinarians also have boarding facilities. If using this type of accommodation, find out if sick cats are kept in the same area as those being boarded. Insist on seeing the boarding area before leaving your cat at an animal clinic. As many viruses are airborne, animal hospitals are likely places for your cat to pick up diseases if sick cats are housed in the same room.

If your cat has a special bed or rug, be sure to leave it with the cat. A familiar object with your scent on it is reassuring to the cat in strange surroundings. Most cats appreciate having a favorite toy with them. Food and water dishes are provided.

On arrival make sure the proprietor records your home address as well as a temporary one in case of emergency. It is wise to leave written particulars in the cat's diet, food and drug allergies, habits and any medication that is to be given. Include the name, address and telephone number of your veterinarian on this list. You will probably be asked to sign a consent to medical treatment form along with an agreement stating that, if the cat should become ill and a veterinarian called to give treatment, you understand such treatment is at your expense.

Before leaving, see that the cat has been safely installed. Most adult cats take a day or two to settle down and happily accept their stay.

DECLAWING A CAT

Many people, including the majority of the veterinary profession, feel that declawing is cruel and unnatural for the cat. Some say that as long as it is correctly performed, it is not a cruel procedure.

Correctly done, declawing is permanent. Onychectomy or declawing is the surgical removal of the claw, including the germinal cells responsible for growth and all or part of the terminal bone of the toe. The toe is extended and the bone and ligaments are severed at or just after the last joint. Wrongly performed, the pad can be cut or misshapen claws may regrow.

The cat's ability to climb and defend itself are greatly reduced. For this reason, I oppose declawing. A declawed cat has no protection from other animals if attacked when allowed outside. Even if the cat is not allowed outside, there is always the risk the cat will escape or sneak out behind your back.

There are other alternatives to declawing. Keep the cat's nails trimmed on a regular basis. Provide a scratching post and train the cat to use the post and not your furniture. Cats are easy to train if you take the time.

The thin cat does not get enough food and the fat cat is the result of overfeeding.

3

Feeding the Cat

PROPER NUTRITION is essential to the general well-being and health of your cat. The three basic factors that influence the longevity, appearance and mental attitude of a cat are genetics, proper care and nutrition. If any of these factors are missing, then the possibility of your cat reaching its genetic potential is slim.

Cats are carnivores. In the wild they are able to balance their diet naturally by ingesting the vegetable matter from the digestive systems of their prey. Cats that are allowed outdoors usually supplement their diets by hunting. A cat confined indoors is dependent upon its owner for a balanced diet. While many of its requirements are not too different from those of humans, it is important that you do not feed your cat according to your own particular tastes and needs.

Cats can tolerate a wide variety of foods, and many people feel that a great variety is necessary in a cat's diet. People sometimes go to astonishing extremes to attain that variety. These misconceptions are based on personal opinion and preference, rather than on scientific study. Gourmet or exotic diets are not necessary for your feline. A plain, wholesome food manufactured especially for cats has proven to be the best.

By studying the feral cat, who thrives by eating very few types of food, we can see that an elaborate diet is unnecessary for the household cat. Our principal interest should focus on quality of the diet and not quantity of variety.

While some owners overelaborate the cat's diet, others go to the opposite extreme by training their cat to demand one particular type of food. You should provide a meal that is varied enough to satisfy all the cat's nutritional needs.

The feral cat is able to balance its diet naturally.

James Curtis

Ensure that the variety is the same as in a meal of natural prey. That is variety in one meal.

Beside the proper balance of the cat's diet, it is important to give the animal sufficient quantities. The cat must receive enough food to furnish energy for its daily living. This energy in food is measured by burning it in calorimeters to see how many heat units or calories it holds. We know how many calories a resting cat needs. The more the cat exercises or works, the more calories it needs. Living, playing, working or exercising all require energy that is extracted from food. If a cat does not get enough to eat, then it will live on stored fat and grow thin. If it eats too much, the surplus will be stored as fat or be discarded in the feces. All cats use the greatest amount of their energy intake to maintain the functioning of body systems and to keep warm. Muscular activity and growth use only a small amount of energy intake.

Cats need water, mineral, amino acids, fatty acids and vitamins along with enough food. A well-fed cat is not a fat cat, but a fat cat is a badly fed cat. Mealtimes are a big event in your cat's life.

BALANCED DIETS

What is a balanced diet? The odor, taste and consistency of food influences the cat's taste. Commercial food products range from the moist, canned variety to semimoist in plastic packs to dry meal. The cat needs a variety of foods for total health.

Most cat foods are scientifically formulated and balanced, providing calories for energy and nutritional elements for body building. Vitamins, minerals, fatty acids, protein, fat and carbohydrates are added in the proper proportions. When you add extras, you run the risk of upsetting this balance.

Even though domestic cats live and thrive on commercially prepared cat food, some owners prefer to use a diet of fresh foods. When the owner is feeding several cats, this method may be more economical but it also makes achieving a balanced diet more difficult.

Variety is the cardinal rule when using a diet of fresh foods. By eating too much raw meat, your cat does not get enough minerals, vitamins and carbohydrates. Too much fat, while satisfying caloric requirements, does not provide essential elements. Cereal grains give the necessary bulk fiber and carbohydrates. Yeast, corn, soybean or wheat provide essential fatty acids, along with vitamin B. The proper proportions of calcium, sodium, iodine, phosphorus and choline come from bone meal. Your cat must have the necessary assimilable proteins as well.

Feeding boned fish, muscle meats and poultry exclusively will lead to bone disease, stunted growth and poor eyesight because these foods lack calcium and vitamin A. Too much liver results in vitamin A poisoning. This vitamin, unlike others, is stored in the body and not excreted. To maintain a balanced diet, give meat and liver in a five-to-one ratio, provided extra calcium is supplied.

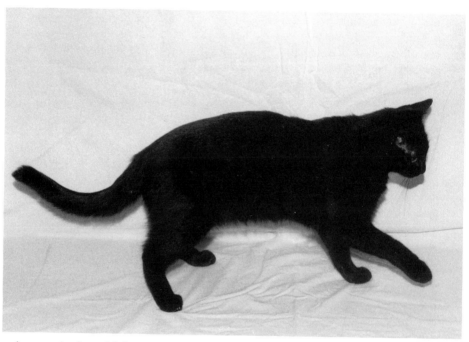

An example of a well-fed cat.

James Curtis

Cats need a high-quality protein such as that found in liver and meat. A low-quality protein that contains a great deal of connective tissue is poorly utilized. Overcooked foods contain denatured proteins that are not absorbed.

Certain fish are nutritionally dangerous when used overabundantly in the diet. Tuna and other oily fish rich in polyunsaturated fats lead to a disease known as yellow fat disease. These fish destroy vitamin E through an oxidation process. An excess of horsemeat has the same effect on the cat.

Some raw foods contain harmful substances unless cooked. For example, raw fish contains an enzyme causing a vitamin deficiency and can carry germs that cause infections. Raw egg whites contain a substance that destroys vitamin B, but will provide valuable protein, vitamins and fat when cooked with the yolks.

Bones should be minced after cooking to ensure that a piece of bone does not lodge in the throat or intestinal tract and intestines. Omit the use of fish bones entirely and use a calcium supplement. Vegetables are best when given cooked. Cats do not properly digest raw vegetables.

Water

Water is important to almost every body function of the feline. Seventy-five percent of the cat's body is made up of water. Cats take in approximately one ounce of water per pound of body weight per day, mostly from commercial canned food. The cat's need for a daily supply of fresh water is great, but should water be restricted for some reason, the cat has the ability to retain water.

Milk is one of the first foods most people want to give their cat. Milk is not water, although it is a fluid. If a cat has milk before it all the time, it will need little else. A cup of milk contains half a cat's nutritional requirements. When you give your cat all the milk it wants, you will find it very difficult to alter its diet. Use milk as an occasional treat and not as a substitute for water.

Nearly all the water a cat drinks is absorbed. About 20 percent passes out with respiration and the remainder is excreted in the urine. Water acts as a solvent or vehicle, and very little is used in combination with other substances.

Minerals

Some of the uncombined chemical elements are called minerals. A chemical element is a substance, made up of atoms, that cannot be decomposed by chemical means. These elements may be solid or gases. The cat's nutrition consists of combinations of elements. Minerals compose approximately 6 percent of the cat's body.

Calcium and phosphorus are two of the most important dietary minerals. The cat needs these two minerals in approximately equal amounts to have a correct balance in the body.

Calcium is an essential ingredient for building bones and teeth. Kittens that are raised with a diet that lacks enough calcium grow up to have small, weak bones. This mineral is involved in the action of muscles. It also aids in the clotting of blood. Animal products and bones are a rich source of calcium.

Proteins and Amino Acids

Another group of essentials needed in the cat's diet are proteins. These complex chemicals contain the element nitrogen as a component as well as amino acids. Proteins differ according to the amino acid content.

Various foods have proteins in unequal proportions. Milk proteins have all the essential amino acids. Corn is not complete, therefore is less valuable as a food. Proteins can be mixed to produce a complete assortment of the necessary amino acids. Cornmeal, horsemeat, alfalfa with wheat or oat flour, milk and cereals are compatible mixtures.

Nearly all commercially prepared cat foods contain over 20 percent protein mixtures. The amount of protein found on cat food labels indicates the protein content. Unfortunately, not all of this protein is digestible or usable by the cat. An example of this is the addition of blood meal. While the blood meal increases the protein content, little of it can be absorbed by the cat. Look for cat foods that list "available proteins."

The cat uses protein primarily for body building. Some protein is burned as energy, with the nitrogen being excreted in the urine. Protein foods are not primary energy foods. By feeding a diet of only liver, kidneys, chicken, or muscle meat, you will contribute to your cat's ill health.

Carbohydrates

Cats convert vegetable starch to animal starch, and have the ability to convert protein into glycogen as well. Starch can be found in liver and muscle meat as glycogen. This form of starch is soluble in water.

Fasting depletes stored glycogen in the cat's body. Eating will rapidly replenish these glycogens. Within a few hours of eating, starch can be found stored in the cat's liver. Glycogen changes into blood sugar or glucose as it is circulated for nourishment.

Cats lack the salivary and other enzymes that humans have that are necessary to break down starches. Care should, therefore, be taken in feeding starchy foods such as potatoes or carrots to cats. These foods must be cooked and mashed in order to break down starches to a form that is usable by the cat.

Lactose or milk sugar is found in its natural form in milk. Lactose is the source of acidophilus bacteria in the intestines or in such foods as yogurt cultures. Lactose is easily dissolved by the cat's digestive juices and also acts as a laxative.

Fats

Fatty acids are a combination of many components. Unlike proteins, they have no nitrogen in their composition. As far as we know, only three of these fatty acids are essential to the cat's health. These are all common in nature.

When provided with a healthy, balanced diet, a normal cat's body can get everything it needs from the food it eats.

James Curtis

A cat stores fats in its body in largely the same form as when eaten. As the fat is needed, it is converted into energy.

Fats have the ability to emulsify, acting as a vehicle to carry some vitamins. Mineral oil can absorb them from food in the intestine and prevent absorption. Fat aids in the slowing down of the digestive process to render it more complete.

A balanced diet should contain at least 20 percent fat. The cat living on captured prey generally consumes at least 30 percent fat. The amount of fat needed and used by a cat depends largely on the amount of exercise it gets.

Vitamins

Vitamins are another essential element in the cat's diet. A vitamin is a substance found in minute quantities in natural foods. They are necessary to normal nutrition and growth.

Some vitamins are water soluble, while others are destroyed by heat or age. Some are found in foods containing appreciable amounts of fat and are soluble in fat. Some are manufactured synthetically. We know that vitamins are essential only in very small amounts. Most vitamins have individual but similar functions.

FREQUENCY AND AMOUNT

The quantity of food and frequency of feeding your cat is just as important as what you feed it. The amount of food that a cat needs depends on its weight, age, activity, and condition. A growing kitten, pregnant cat or lactating queen needs more calories than a sedentary, housebound elderly feline. Extremes in environmental temperature, stress or illness also increase the calorie requirement.

The best guide is to feed the amount needed to maintain good body weight. Excess of food causes obesity. This is particularly common in neutered cats, due to being overfed by their owners.

The adult cat will generally choose its own mealtimes if enough food is left out during the day. Dry and semimoist foods may be safely left out all day. Canned food will keep only about twelve hours maximum, if it is kept in a cool place and flies are kept from it.

It is best to feed in two separate meals, giving half the daily amount at each feeding. A cat can be trained to eat its meals promptly by removing the food dish after about a half-hour. Always try to feed your cat at the same time every day.

Growing kittens must have several smaller meals during the day. The kitten's stomach is smaller than its head. It is not capable of eating its daily requirement in one or two meals.

The pregnant or lactating queen needs small, frequent meals. She also needs 20 percent more food than a cat that is not in her condition. Adequate milk

Cats should be fed from separate dishes.   *James Curtis*

production depends on her food consumption. Once the kittens are born, give her as much food as she wants until her kittens are weaned.

Adequate milk production depends on the quality and quantity of the nursing queen's diet. During lactation, her caloric requirements are almost 100 percent higher than normal, so it is important that her diet be complete and balanced. Moisten dry food to help increase her intake.

The older cat often gets particular about its food. This is because the sense of smell may diminish in the elderly cat. Cats do not eat if they cannot smell their food first.

Care must be taken not to allow the elderly cat to become dependent on only one type of food. This causes nutritional deficiencies that shorten that cat's life span. Commercially prepared cat foods are the best for the older cat. Milk is a good source of protein for this cat but may cause diarrhea.

Older cats generally need a good vitamin and mineral supplement as both an appetite and hormone stimulant. These supplements should be given under the direction of your veterinarian.

MISTAKES IN FEEDING

Be careful not to overfeed your cat. Some cats are especially good beggars, and it is hard to resist them. Firmness is necessary for their well-being. Obesity is especially hard on the heart in a cat, just as it is in humans.

Cats can be given a treat of table scraps, but use common sense. Never give a cat bones and cartilage. Their sharp teeth will splinter the bones, causing punctures in the intestines. Foods that are too salty, spicy or high in sugar content are not good for a cat either.

If you have more than one cat, each cat should have its separate dish. In this way, all your cats can eat what they need, and if an individual is off color, you will discover it more quickly.

Cats are creatures of habit; therefore, use the same dish at the same location for each meal. Wash the dishes after each use.

The cat's appetite is affected by how its food is prepared and presented. Noise or the presence of strange people will put the cat off its food. A cat has a very keen sense of smell and taste. Food that is slightly stale will generally be refused.

The food temperature is important to a cat. Most seem to prefer food at room temperature or slightly warmer. Do not serve food straight from the refrigerator, but warm it slightly.

A cat's diet should not consist solely of moist foods. Dry foods help clean teeth and gums by removing the tartar buildup. Alternate the moist and dry foods or serve meals of moist food and keep a bowl of dry down at all times and let the cat self-feed. A dry food snack can also be given at bedtime.

The cat that refuses its food may be either sick or overfed. Consult your veterinarian for the proper diet for a sick cat. Proper feeding plays an important role in the recovery process.

Obesity is hard on the cat's heart. *James Curtis*

A cat that does not get enough to eat lives on stored food, growing thin. *James Curtis*

4

The Tom and Queen

In RECENT YEARS, the breeding of purebred cats has increased. The cat is now the most popular type of house pet. This is due to the growing trend of apartment and condominium living. A cat is much more adapted to this life-style than a dog. Today, in many families both the wife and husband work outside the home, therefore the self-sufficient cat seems to be the pet of choice when there is no one home all day to walk the dog.

This increased demand for cats has created an increase in breeding. Many novice cat owners feel there is a profit to be made by breeding cats and want to breed their cat, in order to get a return on their investment. A purebred cat should be mated only to bring out the best characteristics of the breed, with the objective being breed improvement in the offspring.

If you have acquired a purebred female cat and want to breed her, you should first visit and talk to several breeders. They will tell you there is no profit to be made in breeding, but there is a great deal of expense involved. First you must arrange a mating. This often entails transporting the female considerable distances. You will have to pay a stud fee to the owner of the tom. Depending on the pedigree and show awards of the stud, the fee could represent a considerable outlay.

Once your cat is bred and back home, you face the cost of essential veterinary treatment. An expectant mother requires several visits to the veterinarian during her pregnancy. If she has problems during delivery, you could face

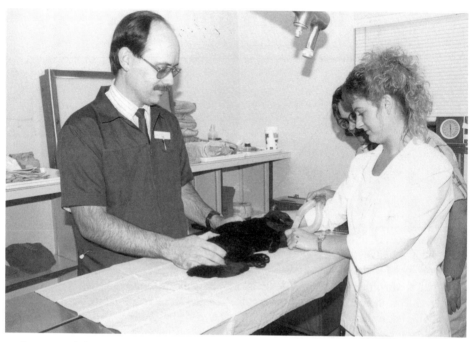

A young male being prepped for surgery.

several hundred dollars in vet bills. In addition you will have costs for equipment, food, showing and advertising.

For your kittens to bring a top price, you must first establish your reputation, and this takes many years. Until then you can expect to average less than two hundred dollars per kitten. The average number of kittens in a litter is four. When you consider the return on your initial investment, you will be in the hole before the kittens are even born. These costs do not include the enormous amounts of your time involved in caring for the mother and babies.

Breeding is more than bringing a male and female together. You need skill, knowledge and a long-term dedication to produce genetically sound, healthy kittens. This takes years of studying genetics and pedigrees. Dedicated breeders consider themselves fortunate if they recover a portion of their costs at the end of the year when they balance their ledgers. The business of breeding and selling cats is complex and certainly not profitable for the amateur.

Some cat owners simply want their children to see the miracle of birth. Libraries and public school systems have excellent films available for educational purposes showing the birth of animals. It is better to allow your children to learn about the miracle of birth from one of these films than to have a litter of kittens that you will regret breeding later.

There are thousands of unwanted kittens euthanized each year in pounds because someone had a litter of kittens that could not find homes. Ask yourself if you really want to add to the overpopulation crisis by breeding your cat.

SPAY/NEUTER

Altering a cat means surgically removing the reproductive organs. This procedure in the female is called spaying. Neutering is the sex-altering operation for the male. When this surgical procedure is performed, the mating urge is neutralized and reproducing is no longer the objective of a cat's life. Other facets of the cat's individual personality emerge. The cat develops an interest in other things. Altered cats are more playful and affectionate. They make their human companions the focal point of their lives.

Cats do not need to experience parenthood before they are altered. The sexual urges are instinctive and are stimulated by the sex hormones in the body. When this stimulus is removed before a sex-behavior pattern has been set by practice, there is no frustration.

Besides producing unwanted litters, the whole male or female is subjected to many medical problems that do not affect the altered cat. The alter tends to be a healthier, happier animal. And it is much easier to care for the altered cat, as you are relieved of the burden of worrying about a female in season or the male wandering.

The altered cat stays close to its home.

James Curtis

TOM OR MALE CATS

A male cat reaches sexual maturity between six and ten months. The normal tom generally has one objective in life. He is constantly looking for a female to receive his loving attention, showing no discretion in his choice of a partner. He vigorously pursues any and all willing, able females he encounters to satisfy his primordial urge.

The male has a powerful sex drive that is foremost in his mind at all times. The whole or intact male not used for stud often becomes nervous and aggressive. He is restless when kept housebound. He frequently yowls at doors and windows to be let out to roam.

The tom will roam to any length to find a female when let out. He is careless about crossing streets, often getting struck by passing cars, risking severe injury and death. He can wander too far from his home and become lost. These cats frequently wind up dead on the side of the road or in shelters.

The tom is prone to fight other males in his pursuit of female companionship. These fights are terrible, characterized by hissing, spitting, clawing, scratching and biting. The male will often return home from his nightly sojourns scratched and bleeding.

Male cats begin to spray as they reach sexual maturity. Spraying is a territorial act done to advertise their presence to a female. This spraying or wetting is the release of an unbearably strong-smelling urine. A male cat will wet on anything that is handy in the house, and the spray will damage anything it comes in contact with, leaving ugly brown stains and a smell that is impossible to remove from drapes, furniture, carpets or walls. Once the habit of spraying in the intact males starts, it is impossible to break.

Stud tail is a condition that affects the intact male. The sebaceous or oil-producing glands in the skin at the base of the tail produce an excess of oil. Dirt gets trapped in the hair, causing a greasy and discolored spot surrounding the tail. These glands can become secondarily infected, requiring antibiotic therapy.

NEUTERING

This neutering of a male is a short simple procedure, done under anesthetic. There is seldom pain, discomfort or complications after this operation. It rarely involves an overnight stay in the hospital. The hairs on the genitalia are shaved and the scrotum is scrubbed with an antiseptic. Two small cuts are made to expose the testicles, which are carefully severed so there is no bleeding or chance for infection. The incision is so small that sutures are generally not necessary. It is allowed to close naturally and heal of its own accord. Neutering is recommended for any male that is not used in a breeding program.

Males should not be neutered before they reach sexual maturity. The ideal time is around eight to ten months, but it may be done at any time in the adult.

The altered cat is not as aggressive as the intact tom.

James Curtis

If done too soon the operation can stunt the cat's growth. Your veterinarian will gladly advise you when it is time to neuter your kitten.

Occasionally after an intact adult is neutered he will continue to spray. A series of female hormone injections and tablets can usually correct this problem. It is best to keep the cat penned or caged for about two to three weeks until the hormone therapy has had a chance to help his system readjust. Following surgery, the urine in the alter loses its strong odor.

This operation negates the many problems associated with strong male sexual behavior, although in the adult cat behavioral changes do not occur instantly. It may take a little more time for the results to become apparent.

The altered male fights less. He will not go racing off after every rival and therefore will be less exposed to danger. He will grow much more affectionate and may even become lazy. The neuter is more home loving, tending no longer to roam, preferring to stay close to home. The neuter seems to be more willing to play with humans and other cats than the intact male. I have four alters that range in age from five years to one year. They play together just like a litter of three-month-old kittens, never fighting.

THE QUEEN OR FEMALE CAT

Reproductive behavior in cats is basically the same as in any other animal except for one significant difference. Unlike most mammals, the female cat is an induced ovulator rather than a spontaneous one. This means that the release of eggs in the female is brought on by copulation. As a result, pregnancy is never a matter of chance. When copulation occurs in a healthy, fertile cat at the right stage of her heat or estrus cycle, the results are inevitable. The sperm and egg unite, making the induced ovulation a biological fact that guarantees impregnation.

It can take several matings to induce ovulation. Impregnation will not stop after one act of copulation; thus a female may have some eggs fertilized by one male cat and some fertilized by another tom.

The female reaches her sexual maturity between six and ten months of age. At this time she has her first heat. These heat cycles are unmistakable. She emits all manner of loud vocalizations or calls to indicate to a male she is ready. Some females have a call loud enough to cause sleepless nights for the owner.

There is a marked change in the queen's behavior patterns while in heat. She rolls madly on the floor, rubs frantically against anything she can find and assumes peculiar postures. Often the tail is lifted and flung to the side, while the hindquarters are raised in the air. The female in season will spray urine all over the house in her attempt to attract a tom. While the female's scent is not as pronounced as the tom's, nevertheless, it will stain and damage just as badly.

A queen is extremely restless just prior to, during and after these heat cycles. It is not uncommon for her to go off her food. The female allowed to experience several cycles without being bred loses weight.

The courtship ritual. *James Curtis*

The queen rolls madly calling for a male.　　　　　　　*James Curtis*

The female cat experiences several heat cycles a year, primarily from early spring to late summer. These cycles normally last for about three weeks and consist of two phases. There are many factors that influence the onset of the heat cycle. Nutrition, environment, temperature, health and the amount of daylight all have an effect on the hormone levels of the queen. Long periods of daylight stimulate hormonal activity. This is nature's method of ensuring the birth of young in the spring. Females housed indoors can be sexually active any time of the year, due to the artificial lighting to which they are exposed.

The time lapse between heat cycles varies in cats. It may be several weeks before a female has her next season or it could be several days. Some queens follow predictable patterns, while others do not. A lactating female usually comes into season when her kittens are a few days old and again when they are around eight weeks. She can become pregnant again while still nursing her current litter.

MATING

The queen that is allowed outside chooses her mate. Cats are definitely not monogamous animals; often a female may choose to mate with several different males. It is entirely possible for one litter of mixed-bred kittens to be sired by more than one tom.

Cats are without inhibitions and are quite willing to mate in the open. They do not seek cover, nor does the presence of humans deter them. It is not uncommon to see several males circling and following a queen in season.

When she is ready, the tom approaches her from behind. He grasps her by the scruff of the neck as he mounts her with his front legs. The queen raises her hindquarters slightly and flings her tail to the side to present her vagina. The male arches his back to position the penis and makes one or two rapid thrusts to achieve penetration.

When copulation is completed, the male leaps away rapidly to avoid being scratched as the queen pulls forward, hissing and clawing. The male retreats to a safe distance to wash. The female rolls over several times, then washes. After a few minutes she may pat the male to signal she is ready and the mating process can begin again.

FEMALE PROBLEMS

The female that is left intact is subject to several reproductive disorders, especially if she is not bred. Some of these disorders are serious and can become life-threatening.

It is not uncommon for a female who is allowed repetitive heat seasons without being bred to develop follicles or small cysts on the ovaries and uterus. These small growths will increase the frequency and duration of her heat cycles.

Flower and her unwanted litter wait in a shelter for adoption.   *James Curtis*

When this happens, the cat becomes nervous and aggressive and loses weight. She may not fully develop to her potential growth.

The intact female is more subject to metritis than is the spay. This is an acute infection of the uterus that flares up after a normal heat season. The symptoms may range from fever and a decrease in appetite to a foul-smelling vaginal discharge. This condition responds to fluid and antibiotic therapy, but your veterinarian is most likely to recommend spaying to remove the infected uterus.

When metritis has progressed to a chronic state, pyometra often follows. In metritis, the uterus fills with pus, the cervix opens, and the pus drains from it. In pyometra, the cervix remains closed, not allowing the release of the purulent fluid. The uterus then fills with this pus. Without the surgical removal of the infected uterus, this condition can be fatal.

The frequency of breast cancer in the intact female is much greater than in the spay. Approximately 80 percent of mammary tumors are malignant. The incidence of cancer is substantially reduced if a cat is spayed.

SPAYING

Since the queen's sexual urges are seasonal, the age at which she is spayed is not as important as it is in the male. The results are the same no matter when the female is altered. The ideal time is around eight to ten months of age unless she is permitted free access outside; then it should be done when she is around six months old. By this time she has her permanent teeth and generally has not experienced a serious season.

Ovariohysterectomy, the surgical procedure for spaying, is a little more complicated than for neutering. The female is placed under general anesthesia, the abdominal cavity is opened and the ovaries and part of the uterus are removed. This requires an incision visible from the outside with several small sutures. Most cats recover rapidly from this procedure without any complications. This procedure is best done between heat seasons and not during one.

There is no truth that a female will be a better cat if allowed to have one litter before being spayed. The fact is, just the opposite is true. Spaying results in a gentler, more even tempered disposition. The spayed female is loving and affectionate to her owner.

The female does not grow fat and lazy when spayed. A fat female is the result of being overfed by its owner and not from being spayed. All animals slow down with age, due to the ticking of the biological clock. Spaying has no effect on this process. A spayed cat is generally more playful because she is more relaxed.

The spayed female does not spray and will no longer experience the heat season. This reduces her tendency to roam in search of male companionship and her constant desire to go outside. She interacts socially with other cats better than the intact female.

Molly, a spay, has no desire to roam but is content to stay home near humans. *James Curtis*

PREGNANCY

The gestation period for a cat is approximately sixty-three days. It is not uncommon to have a variation of sixty-one to sixty-five days. The female shows no outward signs of pregnancy until three to four weeks after she has conceived. At that time the nipples begin to enlarge and change to a brighter pink. They become firmer and more erect. You can feel a fullness in the lower rib-cage area.

The pregnancy can be verified by an experienced veterinarian as early as three weeks from mating. The ideal time for a veterinary checkup is between three to four weeks. At this time the enlargement of the uterus can be felt along with the kittens. They feel like small Ping Pong balls. It is useful to know approximately how many kittens the female is carrying. This manual palpation should not be attempted by an amateur, as clumsy groping and squeezing can seriously damage the kittens and can cause the female to abort the pregnancy. Pregnancy will be obvious by the increase in the size of the queen's abdomen.

Except for a nutritional boost in her diet, the pregnant queen should be allowed to lead a normal life. A healthy cat in peak condition is quite able to cope with her pregnancy without help from you. She can play and climb with safety. She does not need or want to be fussed over by her owner.

Generally no medication is given to a pregnant cat except in an emergency. Never allow a vaccination to be given to a pregnant cat, especially the live feline infectious enteritis or panleucopenia, sometimes called distemper or respiratory vaccine. Both of these vaccines will affect the unborn kittens. Neither should the feline leukemia vaccine be given to a pregnant cat—it may cause the cat to abort or the kittens to be malformed. Steroids and the antibiotic griseo-fulvin, given for ringworm or other fungus, are known to cause deformities.

If the queen experiences constipation, provide natural relief in her diet. Milk often helps, as does a meal of oily fish. If she is carrying a large litter, she may have difficulty cleaning the anal region. If this happens, gently wash the area with warm water and pat dry.

Several days before the kittens are due, the nipples should be cleaned with warm water. This removes the waxy secretions that can build up during pregnancy. If the female is a longhair, it is best to trim the hair away from both the nipples and genital areas.

GETTING READY FOR DELIVERY

About two weeks before delivery, the queen will become restless. She begins to search for a place to have her kittens. She may need a little persuading in selecting the spot you have chosen.

At this time you should provide her with a kittening box. Place a fairly large cardboard box in a protected spot. The box must be large enough to allow the queen to stretch out comfortably. This first box should not be too deep, in case you have to help her and since she likes to be able to see who is approaching

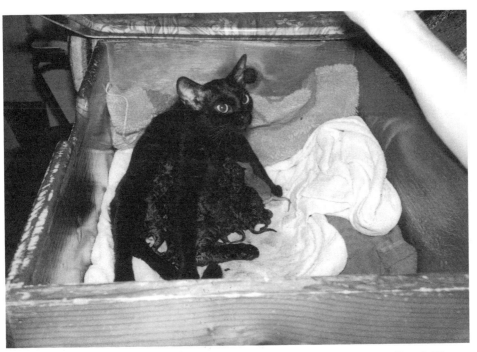

Provide the queen with a large kittening box placed in a warm, secure spot.   *Beverly Dixon*

by just slightly lifting her head over the top. Line the bottom of the box with several layers of newspapers. Until the actual birth, put a soft cloth on top of the papers. A queen likes to knead and arrange this cloth.

When labor begins, remove everything from the box but the newspapers. Newspaper absorbs the fluids that are expelled and can be easily removed to keep the nest warm and dry between the arrival of each kitten. Keep the room containing the kittening box at a steady warm, dry temperature. Dampness and cold are dangerous to newborns and may cause hypothermia. A newborn kitten cannot regulate its body heat properly and will quickly expire if chilled.

There are several items that should be kept close at hand that may be needed during delivery: a jar of petroleum jelly, rubbing alcohol, cotton swabs, several pieces of clean toweling, and a pair of sharp surgical scissors.

After the sixty-first day, watch the queen closely. Keep her indoors until after she gives birth. If she is allowed to wander off, there is a great chance she will deliver her kittens under a house or in a bush. Her behavior indicates birth is imminent, but checking her temperature is a good way of keeping on top of the situation. Take her temperature rectally each day after the sixty-first day. When her temperature has dropped one full degree centigrade from normal, labor should begin in the next eighteen hours. This drop in temperature is due to hormonal changes. The start of milk production is another sign of imminent delivery.

STAGES OF LABOR

At the start of the first stage of labor, the respiration increases. The queen may breathe through her mouth while purring rhythmically. This stage may last for several hours. It is not a cause for worry, and provided the queen is content, do not fuss over her. Offer her some food, but do not be surprised if she refuses.

The fetuses lie within the horns of the uterus at this stage. There is a vaginal discharge as labor proceeds. It is colorless at first but later becomes bloodstained. If it is foul smelling or if bleeding is profuse, consult your veterinarian immediately.

The onset of contractions indicate the second stage of labor. These contractions move the fetuses toward the cervix. The initial contractions may be spaced an hour apart. The rate will increase until just before delivery, when they come about every thirty seconds. The queen will show signs of agitation. Soothe her by gently rubbing her belly and talking to her.

DELIVERY

Soon after the queen's water breaks, you will see the first kitten emerge enclosed in the amniotic sac. The mother will bite this sac to free the kitten and lick its face. This licking stimulates the breathing reflex. If she does not clean this sac after a minute, then you must act quickly to remove the membrane. Rub the kitten dry with a piece of clean toweling to stimulate the newborn to breathe, taking great care not to tear the umbilical cord. Then carefully tear or cut the cord about one inch from the kitten's navel. If the cord bleeds, tie a piece of thread on the tip and place a drop of antiseptic over the open end. After the kitten is clean and breathing, place it, gently, close to the mother's side.

The queen will eat the placenta. This provides her with liquid and nourishment between births. The placenta contains hormones her system needs. In the wild this would be all the nourishment she would have for a few days. It is not necessary for the domesticated cat to eat all the placentas. After she has eaten two, the rest may be discarded. Each kitten has an individual placenta, so make sure they are all accounted for. If left in the uterus they can cause an infection.

After the arrival of all the kittens, clean the box and line it with fresh, dry paper. A soft flannel cloth or piece of sheeting can be used on top to provide some traction for the newborns. Avoid using toweling or other similar loosely woven material, as this type of material can catch a claw, causing a severe tear. Offer the mother some warm milk and food after she is settled.

If the queen has experienced hard labor contractions for two hours and no kittens have emerged, take her to your veterinarian. If you have any doubt, consult him.

Occasionally a kitten's head is too large to pass through the pelvis. If professional help is not given in time, the kitten will die and there is a great chance the others behind it will be lost as well. The dead kitten presents an immediate source of infection to the queen. A Cesarean section must be performed if the litter and mother are to be saved.

There is no way of knowing how long a queen will be in labor. This varies from cat to cat. Some females produce their kittens every fifteen minutes, while others may take one or two hours between kittens. The calmer and quieter you are, the more relaxed the queen will remain. Remember this is a normal process for her, and she can usually do quite well on her own.

5

Raising Kittens

WHEN YOU ACQUIRE a kitten, you are also getting an adult cat. In a year the kitten will be an adult. The kind of adult it becomes depends on its genetic background as well as the care you give it during the growing process.

Most people just want their kitten to be a lovely pet and have no interest in entering it in competition at a show. Any cat, whether it is a pet or a show cat, deserves the best human attention possible. The kitten that receives the benefit of this extra individual love and attention will stand a better chance of developing to its full potential.

The queen or mother has the responsibility of the care and training of her babies. The bond between the tom and queen becomes weak or nonexistent after mating. Feline society, unlike human society, does not demand that the father support his mate or offspring; instead the queen is on her own. If the queen is a good mother, the kittens generally survive. The stray cat is almost always an excellent mother. She will satisfy every need of her kittens and never abandon them. She is their sole provider and teacher.

THE NEWBORN

Newborn kittens should not be touched or handled by strangers. The queen can be disturbed by an unfamiliar scent and not recognize the kitten as her own. When this happens, she will refuse to allow it to nurse.

Larry Johnson

The queen is a devoted mother and lavishes almost all her attention on her kittens for the first few days, leaving them only long enough to take care of her nourishment and toilet needs. If possible, place her litter pan close to the nursery, as she does not like to wander far from her kittens. She will eat much better if she is fed near the newborns.

The queen will sleep less than normal during this period. Kittens must take milk during their first twenty-four hours in order to survive. A good mother will encourage her litter to nurse frequently, and will nap briefly between nursing periods.

Once the kittens are born, do not move the location of the kittening box. If you do, the mother may not like the new place and will begin to carry the newborns about the house, dumping them in various hiding places. Should the mother begin to move her kittens, there may be several reasons behind her behavior. She may feel the location is too light or dark. She may think it too hot or cold for the well-being of her offspring. She may sense for some reason her babies are in danger from too much handling or viewing. And if there is not enough room in the kitten box for her to comfortably stretch out to nurse the kittens, she will move them to a new location. Cats are naturally good mothers and act for good reasons. One who neglects or moves her young generally has a good reason. You should attempt to find out what is disturbing her and try to correct the problem.

A new mother needs privacy and peace. She should be left in a semidarkened room with her new family to rest. She needs to establish a tranquil mood to prepare herself for the reflexive release of milk when her kittens begin to nurse. Keep a watch to make sure she is feeding the kittens properly. A first-time mother bewildered by her new responsibilities may not stay with her kittens unless you are there with her. Should this happen, encourage her to stay in the box. If she won't cooperate, then you must make sure the kittens are kept warm. Place a heating pad or hot water bottle inside the box to keep them warm and dry. Usually this phase passes after a day or two.

Kittens are born with a rooting reflex and usually scramble wildly at first for their food source. The mother will gently lick and nuzzle them to guide them to her side. When kittens begin to nurse they wrap their tongues tightly around the nipple, holding almost continually for the first day or two. While nursing, they knead the queen's breasts to stimulate the flow of milk.

The first milk is called *colostrum*. It is composed of fats, lactose, casein and various nutrients. Colostrum is very high in antibodies and is the newborn kitten's first source of immunity to contagious diseases. This first milk cleanses the digestive tract and initiates intestinal activity along with providing nutritional needs.

A well-fed kitten is quiet, with the middle of its body turgid and nicely rounded. Newborn kittens spend most of their time sleeping. A group of crying kittens indicates something is amiss. If the mother is not sitting on them, then they may not be getting enough milk. Make sure they are able to find the nipples. Check to see if the mother is producing milk by gently squeezing the nipple.

A proud mother with her family.

Larry Johnson

A queen cares totally for her kittens the first few days.

James Curtis

Do not assume a mother will have no milk. Some queens may take several hours following the birth of a litter for a milk supply to become established. If you exercise patience and leave the mother and her babies alone for a short time, the kittens will start to suck and the milk will come. Kittens will be fine without food for a few hours. It is important they receive the colostrum before the milk. Do not be too hasty to start supplementary feeding.

If the mother has not begun to produce milk for eight to twelve hours after birth, then it is necessary to supplement by hand feeding. I use a mixture of half evaporated milk and water with a teaspoon of Karo syrup, given with an eye-dropper or doll-size baby bottle. The amount of food will vary according to the size of the kitten. The rule of thumb is to feed according to their appetite needs.

After feeding, rub the abdomen and genitals gently with a damp cotton ball to induce urination and defecation. Do not repeat this supplemental feeding for at least five hours. If the kittens are fed too much they will be satisfied and not make an effort to nurse from their mother; she must be suckled in order to produce sufficient milk. But the kittens should not be allowed to get weak from starvation. If the mother still is not producing milk, your veterinarian can give her an injection to stimulate lactation.

Once the mother is successfully nursing, keep a watch on her nipples. If one becomes blocked, it will cause the gland to become inflamed. Occasionally a kitten may bite the nipple, initiating an abscess. If the queen cries when the kittens nurse or she stands up to feed them, this may indicate trouble with the mammary glands or nipples.

A blocked nipple causes swelling and redness over the gland. A hard, painful lump usually means an abscess. Application of warm, moist heat coupled with antibiotics will relieve the condition. If left untreated, this condition will cause a rapid high fever, endangering the cat's life.

ORPHAN NEWBORNS

A young kitten needs a mother for survival if possible. Newborn or very young orphan kittens without the birth mother or with a mother who is unable to give milk should be put with a substitute mother or wet nurse. Your veterinarian can help you find another mother cat to take the babies. Most nursing queens will readily accept orphan kittens if you rub the smell of her own babies on the orphans.

When putting orphan kittens with a substitute mother, offer the kitten to her bottom first. A mother cat cannot resist or ignore a rear to clean. Place the kitten in the nest for her to find. The crying of an orphan arouses her maternal instinct, and she will take it to her to nurse without question. The kittens can be returned to you once they are weaned.

The primary need of newborn kittens is to be dry and warm. They should be dried thoroughly and placed in a small deep box or basket, lined with warm cloth. A heating pad or hot water bottle can be placed inside to help keep them

Weaning may begin when the kittens are between three and five weeks old. *James Curtis*

warm. Be careful, though, that they do not get too hot. If you are using a hot water bottle, make sure it is wrapped in toweling or similar material to prevent the kittens from being burned.

Newborns require very little milk at first. The mixture of canned milk and water can be used. Give a few drops every hour or two around the clock. Do not feed a newborn kitten that is too weak to swallow. A kitten that is unable to swallow will drown if fed. Kittens will gain in strength without being fed for several hours providing the environment is kept warm. This strength comes from the glycogen stored in the liver before birth. Many newborns have been lost from overanxious feeding before the swallowing mechanism was strong enough to function.

For the first two weeks feed newborns on a two-hour basis. After that reduce the schedule to every three hours. When they reach three to four weeks of age, you can begin to introduce the same solid food diet as kittens being weaned from the nursing mother.

THE FIRST DAYS

All kittens are born blind and deaf, but with a well-developed sense of smell. The newborn is very dependent on its nose. The kitten will find its way to the mother's nipple by smell. A kitten will mark the area around the nipple with its own odor soon after it begins to suckle and will always prefer to use that same nipple.

Territorial marking by smell starts early in the kitten's life. It learns to recognize the boundaries of the nest by smell. If the kitten is removed from the nest, it will try to find its way back by sniffing for a familiar odor.

The mother takes care of her kittens totally for the first three weeks. She will bathe and groom them daily. She licks the hindquarters in order to stimulate the release of urine and feces. Failure of her to do so would quickly cause the death of the kittens at this critical stage.

She will wake them frequently by curling around them to present her nipples, then lick and nuzzle the whole litter. This encourages them to eat. Approximately 70 percent of her time is spent nursing for the first few days.

The eyes will begin to open between eight and ten days. Kittens need to be kept in a dark place until the eyesight is fully developed. Gradually increase the amount of light exposure. If matter collects in the eyes or the lids stick together, bathe the eyes with a cotton ball soaked in a solution of one teaspoon boric acid to eight ounces of warm water. About the same time the eyes open, the first set of teeth begin to appear. Generally, by the end of two weeks kittens have their full complement of senses.

The queen will start leaving the kittens for short periods when they are a few days old. She will be alert to their every move, responding to the sounds rather than the sight of her kittens. Smell, touch and warmth are critical senses to very young kittens. Any disturbance or removal from the nest results in an

Kittens' behavioral elements combine into ever-changing sequences of events. *Larry Johnson*

intense cry. A mother cat will respond to these cries, using them to find her babies.

THE TODDLER

By the time kittens are three or four weeks old, they begin to develop some independence. This change in them will modify the queen's behavior and responses. She will leave the nest more frequently and for longer periods of time. She will sit near them rather than with them upon her return.

The kittens start to initiate feeding by responding to the feeling of hunger. They will go to their mother to nurse, often ambushing her. At this point she will start a gradual withdrawing from them.

At this age they begin to emerge from the nest. They will follow behind their mother, as well as run about to play with each other. As they become mobile, the mother will retreat to a high place where she can oversee her offspring. The queen will call and chirp to any kitten who strays from her sight as she quickly comes to fetch it.

As the kittens grow, the mother will look for a new site for her nest. She will grasp each kitten by the scruff of the neck and carry it to the new nest. In the wild kittens are introduced to solid food at this time; therefore the choice of a nest is influenced by the availability of a food source. The domesticated cat will still move her litter, even though she has no need to follow a food source for her offspring.

Kittens may be started on food between three and five weeks. The best guide on when to start plate feeding is the queen. When she begins to back off from nursing, she is trying to wean her babies. Another guide is watching to see if the teeth are beginning to injure her nipples. When giving solid foods, do not overfeed kittens, as this will cause indigestion and diarrhea. Once indigestion is acquired it is not easily cured. During the weaning process, kittens will still nurse the mother to some extent. If the litter is large, you may begin weaning as soon as the kittens are able to stand on their own, to relieve the burden placed on the lactating queen.

The principle of weaning is to gradually replace the mother's natural milk with an adult diet that will carry the young ones the remainder of their lives. This must be done without upsetting tiny digestive systems. The first food should be milk based.

Start feeding young kittens a soupy mixture of half evaporated canned milk and half water with a teaspoon of Karo syrup. After the first day or so, add a small amount of baby rice cereal and vitamins. As they learn to lap, gradually increase the consistency of this mix. After a couple of weeks, slowly add a small bit of junior baby meat or canned cat food, decreasing the cereal and milk until they are eating a diet of canned food. Any reputable milk preparation for human babies may be used.

Start with two small meals of milk mix a day, then gradually increase to

Larry Johnson

four small meals a day while the kittens are still nursing. Give two meals of the cereal and milk mix and two with meat added to the cereal. It is essential that these meals are kept very small.

Once the mother stops nursing, increase to five small meals. Give two mixed with meat and three with the cereal-milk mixture. Kittens tend to be gluttons if not kept well in check. Also, they eat and lap at individual rates, so care must be taken that each gets the proper amount of food. Never feed kittens between meals.

The queen does not like to clean the hindquarters after solid food is eaten. As soon as plate feeding begins, a litter tray must be provided. The pan should be placed close to the feeding area. After the kitten finishes eating, put it in the tray; it does not take long to litter-train the kittens.

As kittens learn to eat from a plate, you may notice their weight increase slows down or stops. This is normal, and a regular rate of weight gain should return by the time they are nine to ten weeks old.

At around five to eight weeks, if the kittens show signs of indigestion, loose stools, vomiting or ulcerated tongues or if they suddenly refuse to nurse, and you know your plate feeding is blameless, it is better to remove the mother entirely. A young mother that becomes thin or exerts herself too much in producing milk often produces milk that is of unsuitable composition near the end of lactation. The kittens should return to normal at once. If not, consult your veterinarian.

Table I. Kitten Feeding Program

Age in Weeks	Milk Feeds	Meat Feeds	Size in Teaspoons
0–3	0	0	0
3–4	3	0	1/2–1
4–5	3	1	1–2
5–6	2	2	2–3
6–8	2	2	3
8–12	2–3	2	3–4
12–16	2	2	6–8
16–24	1	2	9–12
24–over	0	2	12

LEARNING NEW SKILLS

The waking hours of a kitten appear to be devoted solely to play except at mealtimes. This play has a serious purpose. It is through play that a kitten develops the skills, judgment and behavior necessary to sustain it as an adult. At the same time its body is developing to keep up with behavioral needs.

Feline mothers are noted for being excellent teachers. The most important skill she will teach her kittens is hunting. If a litter pan is provided, she will also quickly teach them to use it. Scientific studies have shown that young kittens have the ability to master such complex tasks as opening a door latch or negotiating physical obstacles when first given a demonstration by their mother.

A kitten has the potential for a vast repertoire of behaviors. The expression of a cat's potential is molded by its early experiences as the individuality of the kittens develops during the first few weeks of life. The mother generally provides the necessary stimulation that promotes this development. Human contact and handling is an effective supplement to this development. Experiments have shown that kittens handled for a minimum of ten minutes a day for the first thirty days developed faster than kittens that did not receive handling.

Handling and general stimulation seems to affect the pituitary gland, adrenal gland and brain. These are the body parts involved with stress reaction. A kitten that is handled is less emotional, more playful and more adept at learning and exploring than one that is not. Kittens that are not handled grow up to be overfearful and more aggressive in their dealing with other cats or people. These skills and attitudes are learned within the first few months. Behavioral skills missing in the kitten are generally lost forever. Kittens need the opportunity to play with others, as this is how they acquire the skills to react and relate to other cats.

Scientific studies have shown that play is common to mammals but rare in cold-blooded vertebrates. The most intelligent and sociable species are the most playful. Play provides the means by which the social skills can be explored and learned. During periods of play, kittens are taught their survival skills by the queen. Physical exercise is another benefit of play. Kittens raised in social isolation and deprived of play grow up to be social misfits unable to properly react to others as well as poor hunters.

At three weeks play takes the form of rough-and-tumble rushing and pouncing. Kittens play with both their littermates and mother. They are learning the territorial and dominant behavior of adulthood. As they grow older, more elaborate play patterns will emerge.

Kittens are delightful to watch when they are stalking, chasing and pouncing on imaginary mice and birds. Their behavioral elements are combined into an ever-changing sequence of events. These signals when given by adults have a serious meaning, but are recognized as play behaviors in kittens. An arch-backed, hissing, spitting kitten is not considered to be a serious threat by its

Feline mothers are noted for being excellent teachers.

James Curtis

littermates. The swats and bites delivered by kittens at play are inflicted with less vigor than as adults engaged in a real fight.

SEPARATION

The queen generally is not upset for more than a day or so when kittens are removed at around six to eight weeks of age, but the kitten may call for its mother for several days. A mother will usually fail to recognize her kittens if they are brought back several months later. A mother allowed to keep her kittens continues to demonstrate maternal behavior toward them even after the kittens become adults.

It is best not to separate kittens from their mother for the first three months. Kittens taken away too early will not fully develop their social skills.

Separation is best accomplished when the queen is eating or otherwise away from her young. Try to remove the kittens one at a time on different days in order to slowly facilitate the queen's return to normal life. A mother will not generally display any possessive reaction if the kittens are removed from her presence after they are ten to twelve weeks old.

Before placing kittens in new homes, a trip to your veterinarian is in order for them. At this time he will give them a thorough health examination along with deworming and the required kitten shots.

6

Feline Diseases

THE PRIMARY CONCERN of a cat owner should be maintenance of the cat's health and well-being. There is a great deal that you can do to prevent illness and accidents to your pet by taking common-sense precautions toward its welfare. Your cat can live a happy, healthy life if you adapt the same type of normal measures you take for keeping yourself healthy.

Proper care requires a fundamental knowledge of hygiene, sanitation and diseases. Be alert to the signs of possible trouble and seek prompt professional advice from a qualified veterinarian whenever necessary. He or she can play an important role in helping you maintain a healthy cat.

CONSULTING A VETERINARIAN

In the past twenty-five years there has been a remarkable advance in the diagnosis and treatment available in veterinary medicine. A broad range of drugs and vaccines has been developed to combat disease, manufactured under the same exacting requirements as those used for humans. Modern surgical techniques applied to the cat are now commonplace. Improved anesthesia and aseptic methods have been combined to increase the chances of successful surgery.

Seeing a veterinarian for a checkup is one of the first things you need to do after bringing your new kitten home. At this first visit, you become acquainted with the veterinarian, and he or she will get to know your pet. The veterinarian will discuss the kitten's development with you along with steps to keep it healthy.

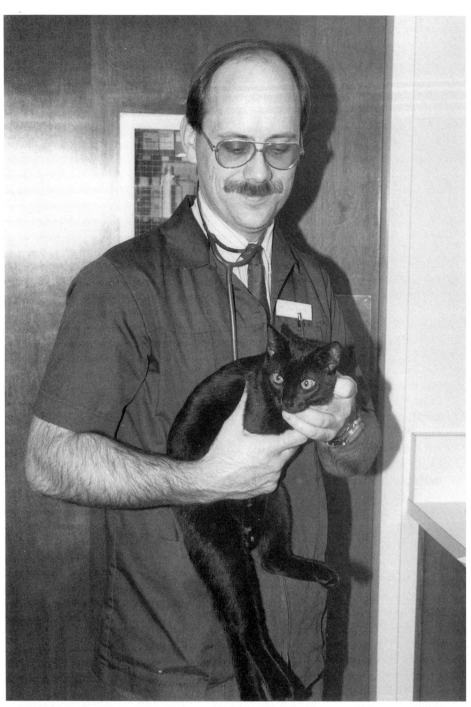

Next to the people in a cat's home, the veterinarian is a cat's best friend. For good health and a long, trouble-free life, regular visits to your veterinarian are essential for your cat. *James Curtis*

VACCINATIONS

The single most important tool of preventive medicine is the vaccination. Your cat should be routinely inoculated against all possible diseases with which it may come in contact. The cost of the vaccination and the risk are relatively small compared to the cost of treatment should your cat become infected with a preventable illness.

Most counties have ordinances requiring that all cats be vaccinated yearly against rabies. Your veterinarian will be able to advise you of the local laws regarding rabies vaccination.

Your veterinarian will recommend that the cat be vaccinated against feline distemper, feline leukemia and the upper respiratory diseases. A cat has the ability to produce protective antibodies against antigens. These antigens are the disease-producing agents. Inoculation by a vaccine makes use of this ability by introducing into the cat's system antigens that are either dead or weakened. They no longer can cause disease but will trigger the production of antibodies. It is by this means that protection against the disease can be achieved. For the immunization to be fully effective a kitten must be healthy, free of parasites and at least eight to twelve weeks old.

PREVENTING ACCIDENTS

Traumatic injuries are more frequent in the cat that is allowed to run outside. This is the best reason to keep your cat indoors. There is basically nothing you can do to prevent or lessen its natural inquisitiveness. Street accidents are the most common, occurring more at night. If the cat is allowed out after dark, supervise its late-night toilet.

The most common indoor calamity is accidental poisoning. The cat is very curious and investigates anything new it sees. Be careful not to leave any type of pesticide, disinfectant or toxic substance where your cat can find it. A cat's habit of licking its paws and fur puts it in danger from household chemicals. A harmless substance becomes highly toxic due to a cat's poor ability to neutralize and excrete poisons.

Many common house plants are poisonous to the cat. A cat is especially attracted to those varieties with shiny leaves or trailing vines and tendrils. Do not place hanging baskets where your cat can reach the leaves. Poinsettias, while lovely to use for Christmas decorations, are highly toxic to your cat.

DIAGNOSING THE SICK CAT

Departure from good health is generally accompanied by observable changes in the cat's responses and body activities. These signs and symptoms require the expertise of a veterinarian to diagnose and treat. The information provided on the following pages is to help you better understand the causes of disease, not to teach you to diagnose or treat the cat yourself.

To know the signs and symptoms of a sick cat, one must first understand the signs of a healthy cat. The healthy cat will have clear, bright eyes. The coat has a lustrous sheen and lies close to the skin. The cat will have a normal appetite, taking an active interest in the world around it, responding normally to external stimuli. The gums are light pink with clean white teeth. The ears are absolutely clean and the nose dry and cool. The skin is dry and smooth.

The average heart rate for the adult is 80 to 175 beats per minute; for the older cat 80 to 150; and for the kitten 150 to 200. A cat's breathing should be quiet and regular, averaging thirty to forty breaths per minute for the kitten; twenty to thirty for the adult cat and twenty for the older adult. The normal temperature is 100 to 102.5°F. The urine in a healthy cat is clear and yellow. The feces should be moist and soft, being dark gray to brown in color.

Symptoms of illness vary according to the type of disease and the stage reached. A sick cat often loses its appetite and refuses food. The eyes look dull, with the haw or third eyelid seen as a film covering the eye. The coat becomes dull and tacky. A sick cat will lie listless or sit hunched up, staring dully, not responding to voice or touch, and it may try to hide in a dark place. A bad mouth odor and gums that are too pale or red indicate problems.

Additional symptoms such as sneezing, vomiting and coughing may be present. Watch for loose stools, diarrhea, blood or mucus in the feces. Discharge from the eyes or nose is not normal. Observe for rapid, shallow or labored breathing. Note any signs of swelling, tenderness or pain. Be very gentle if you have any reason to suspect pain, for the cat may react violently by biting out of instinct.

Be aware of the possible illnesses that can affect your cat, but at the same time try to be objective. There is not necessarily a disease for every symptom. A refusal to eat, in an otherwise healthy-appearing cat, may be caused by change in diet, routine or environment. Diarrhea alone can be an allergic reaction to an item in the diet and is quite common when feeding milk. In a multi-cat family, the occasional vomiting may be caused by hairballs, especially in long-haired breeds. A thorough evaluation of your cat should tell you when to seek the advice of your veterinarian, but when in doubt it's best to call.

EXTERNAL PARASITES

These are small, often microscopic organisms that live by feeding on the skin and hair of the cat. They may transmit other diseases along with opening the door for other infections. Some are blood-suckers, causing severe anemia, while others produce toxins. Regular grooming serves as early warning of infestations. Seek medical advice from your veterinarian, as many parasites produce similar signs.

Fleas

Fleas are a common, perennial problem causing intense irritation and discomfort. The flea is a carrier of the tapeworm. Under favorable conditions, such as the modern dry, centrally heated house, they multiply rapidly. Severe flea infestation if left untreated will cause anemia and even death.

Flea bites produce small reddish patches. Repeated bites may cause an allergy to flea saliva, which is the most common skin disease in cats. The skin will be covered in small pimples with a hard, dry crust. The cat will continuously lick and bite the affected area, causing it to become raw and hairless, resulting in ulcerated sores that are difficult to treat.

Fleas are easily treated by bathing with a flea shampoo containing pyrethrum every three days for two weeks. Powder the cat thoroughly with a commercial cat flea preparation on the days you don't bathe the animal. Treat the bedding and surroundings with a suitable commercial flea spray. Never powder the kitten under eight weeks of age with an adult flea powder, but use one made specifically for the new kitten. Consult your veterinarian before bathing a kitten under eight weeks of age with any flea shampoo.

Mange Mites

These are minute round or oval parasites provoking a broad range of skin conditions from simple dandruff to bald, crusty patches. Mange is highly contagious to other animals and is transmitted by direct contact or infested bedding and grooming equipment.

Fur Mites

This mite lives in the fur of the cat and causes itching and profuse dandruff. It is contagious to humans and appears as itchy blisters or wheals that progress to dry scaling on the hands, forearms and sometimes chest. Fur mite mange generally responds to a selenium sulfide shampoo once a week for three weeks. All household cats should be treated.

Ear Mites

These mites, relatively common in cats, are not visible to the naked eye. Scratching of the ears and shaking of the head may indicate the presence of these mites. The first symptom usually is a dark brown or black crumbly wax in the ears. These mites are very contagious to other cats.

Ticks

This parasite is not often found on cats because of self-grooming. Weekly dusting with a pyrethrum and piperonyl butoxide powder will help as a deterrent.

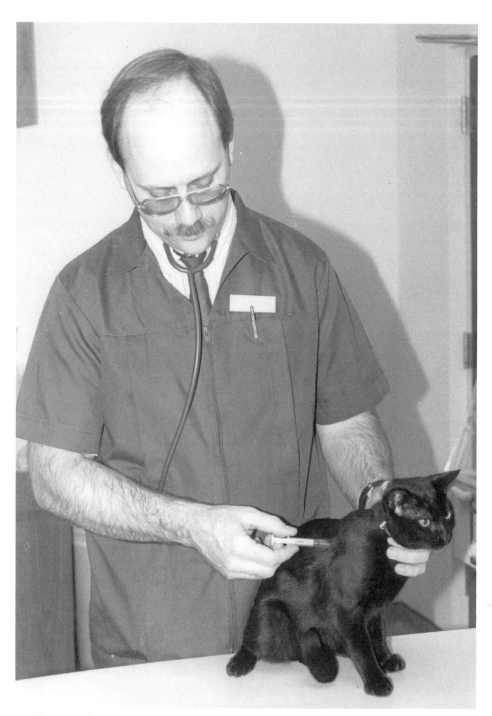

After a cat has gone through all its kitten shots and can be considered an adult, your veterinarian will put it on a program of annual boosters. *James Curtis*

Lice

The well-cared-for cat is highly unlikely to be troubled by lice. These wingless insects are usually present as a symptom of some type of illness, because the cat has become listless and stopped self-grooming. Lice are host specific, and there is no possibility of infecting humans. Lice are spread by direct contact or infected bedding and grooming equipment.

Ringworm

Ringworm is a parasitic fungus spread by direct contact or objects that have been in contact with infected animals and can affect humans. The spores live for years, and it is difficult to eradicate. The fungus grows on the skin's surface, but its toxins are released into the skin, causing itching and inflammation. Symptoms appear two to four weeks after infection and can vary considerably. A Wood's lamp should be used to detect the fungus, as other disorders may produce similar symptoms. Breaks in the skin are accompanied by gray flakes, followed by circular dry, scaly patches. Always wash your hands after treating the infected cat.

Disinfect during and after an outbreak. Burn contaminated bedding. Sterilize all metal or wooden utensils and cages. If you breed or show cats, discontinue sales, cat shows and matings until the infection has been completely eradicated.

ECZEMA

This is a common condition and is a chronic or acute superficial inflammation of the skin. It is caused by improper diet, vitamin deficiencies, hormonal imbalance, allergies and dirty skin. The affected areas will become dry and flaky, turning darker than the rest of the skin.

INTERNAL PARASITES

These organisms may live in the body of the cat. A heavy infestation is highly detrimental to a cat, and some are considered to be human health hazards. Prevention is easy. Most of the internal parasites are worms that spend the early stages of their life cycles in another animal. These can only infect the cat that preys on and eats an infected animal; as a result, outdoor cats are more likely to harbor these parasites. Control external animals that may be hosts and try to prevent your cat from killing and eating prey.

Roundworms

These are thick, white worms that grow to about four inches in length, commonly seen in vomit and feces. Adult worms feed on the digested food in the

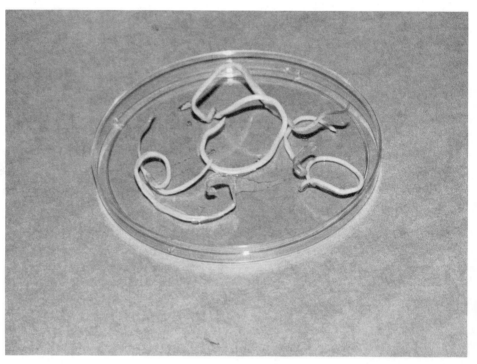

Hookworms.

James Curtis

cat's intestines. The eggs are passed via the feces. A cat picks these eggs up on its feet and fur, getting them into the digestive tract with normal licking. The hatched larvae burrow into the intestinal wall and migrate to the bloodstream and surrounding tissue.

Some larvae get into the abdominal cavity and become dormant. Pregnancy activates the larvae, causing them to migrate into the uterus and infect the unborn kitten. This explains why kittens can have worms when there is no known history of roundworm in the mother.

Fecal examination is the method of detecting the presence of roundworms, but it will only show the adult egg-laying worm that is present in the intestines. If the worms are not in this stage of their cycle, they cannot be diagnosed. Other signs of this parasite may be a swollen belly, loss of weight and shabby coat.

Hookworm

These worms derive their name from the hook-shaped head, which has spines for attachment to the host. They are a problem in hot, humid areas. The cat is infected by swallowing the larvae or from penetration through broken skin. Eggs are passed by feces. The hookworm lives off the small arteries in the intestinal wall, causing severe anemia, weakness and diarrhea. The stool will be dark and occasionally flecked with blood.

The only prevention is to keep the cat indoors, provide clean, dry bedding and change its litter regularly.

Tapeworm

A freshly passed tapeworm resembles a small grain of rice and can be seen in the feces. Infection is acquired by ingesting infected lice and fleas. Tapeworms rob the cat of the food it has eaten, although they are seldom harmful. Symptoms are usually mild diarrhea, reduced appetite, colic, change in coat and nervousness. Treatment is simple but must be combined with control and elimination of fleas if it is to be effective.

Toxoplasmosis

This is a single-cell protozoan parasite and is the most dangerous to humans. The most common method of contracting toxoplasmosis is by eating raw meat, particularly pork. The cat will spread the parasite through infected cysts in the feces.

Generally, the cat is a symptomless carrier. After maturing, the toxoplasma can infect any tissue of the body, producing symptoms that are similar to other diseases. Blood and stool samples are needed to confirm a diagnosis.

This parasite, if transmitted to a pregnant woman, may cause congenital abnormalities to the unborn child. Pregnant women should use caution in handling cats and should never handle soiled cat litter.

This infection can easily be prevented with common-sense methods. Feed only well-cooked fresh meat or heat-processed commercial cat foods. Wash your hands after handling raw meat. Prevent your cat from eating wild prey. Frequent changing and disinfecting of the litter pan reduce the risks of infection.

VIRAL DISEASES

Rabies

This is one of the most feared and dangerous diseases to both animals and humans. It is transmitted by the saliva of an infected animal through a bite or scratch in the skin. All warm-blooded animals can be infected. Always fatal, it causes an agonizing death for the victim.

Once clinical signs have developed, there is no known treatment and cure for animals or humans. Routine vaccination of your cat will give the cat a high degree of protection.

Panleucopenia

Commonly referred to as feline enteritis or feline distemper, it is the most common viral disease affecting cats, claiming more victims than any other disease. Incubation period is about seven days. It is highly contagious to other cats.

Symptoms are usually fever, diarrhea, vomiting, abdominal tenderness, apathy and fluid loss. If not treated immediately, death will quickly follow. This disease causes a decrease of white blood cells. The course of this disease is so swift that it is often mistaken for poisoning. If you suspect this disease, the cat must be rushed to the veterinarian for immediate treatment.

Preventive vaccination is highly recommended.

Leukemia

This virus can be transmitted by cats that appear to be symptomless. The disease takes many different forms. In the most serious cases, swelling in lymph nodes and anemia lead to death. It also weakens the cat's immune system.

Any cat showing symptoms of this disease should be kept in strict isolation, as it is highly contagious to other cats. There is no evidence that feline leukemia is transmissible to humans. There are laboratory tests that detect the presence of this disease and vaccination is the best form of prevention.

Upper Respiratory Infections

There are a number of different viral infections. They are spread through the air or by contact with articles that have been sneezed or coughed upon. The worst of these is pneumonitis, which is a killer.

Symptoms are similar to those of a severe cold in humans. The cat will be feverish, lose its appetite, cough and sneeze. He may have runny eyes, nose and stools. Cats affected by these viruses need intensive care in familiar surroundings. In severe cases, a course of antibiotic therapy and frequent infusion of fluids is the prescribed method of treatment.

Vaccines have been developed for some of the most common strains of pneumonitis. Humans and dogs are not susceptible to these feline respiratory viruses.

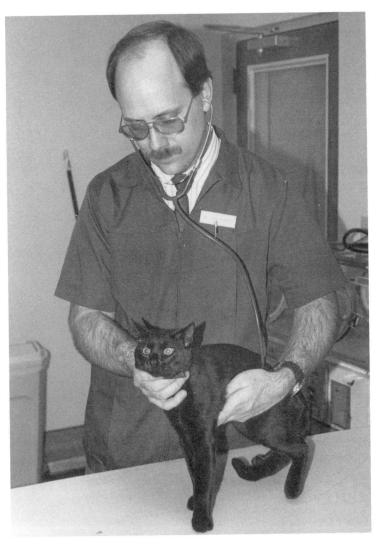

To keep your cat healthy, you should be able to recognize even the smallest symptoms of illness. If your cat appears off-color to you for any reason, have it checked by your veterinarian as soon as possible. *James Curtis*

7

Care of the Sick and Injured Cat

WHEN YOUR CAT is recovering from an illness or surgery, the nursing care you provide will have a vital effect on its recovery. The independence of cats makes for a rather uncooperative patient, requiring a great deal of patience and love from you—the care giver.

Cats have an intense dislike of being medicated or force fed. Their fastidious nature makes them interfere with wounds and dressings. The cat has an innate instinct to hide when ill or hurt; therefore, when nursing the sick animal, do what is necessary for its comfort and well-being but leave it quietly alone as much as possible.

GENERAL CARE

Provide a warm, dry bed for the cat's recovery. The sick cat needs protection from injuring itself. Fill the bed with a soft bedding that is easily laundered. This will help make the animal more comfortable. Place the bed where it is protected from drafts and cold. In the winter a hot-water bottle or heating pad placed under the bed will help keep the cat warm.

A sick cat needs regular grooming like any other. Clean any discharges with a moist, warm cotton ball. Check the hair around the anal and urinary passages. Sick animals often have soft or loose stools. A cat will become distressed if allowed to soil themselves from vomit or feces. If this happens, wash

A sick or new cat should be isolated from the other household cats.   *James Curtis*

the area gently with warm water, then dry the hair as thoroughly as possible. Dust lightly with baby powder or cornstarch, then gently comb.

It is not uncommon for a sick cat to refuse to eat. A cat can survive without solid food for a day or two, but it is vital to prevent dehydration. You may have to administer fluids with an eyedropper or syringe. Give chicken broth, Gatorade, baby cereal or water mixed with sugar or honey. Critically ill cats often respond well to a small amount of Gatorade and homemade chicken broth given every hour or two. It's best if you can coax the cat to eat even the smallest amount on its own rather than having to force-feed a larger amount.

Light, nourishing meals are best, but you may have to feed whatever your sick cat will eat. If the cat's sense of smell is impaired, it may be tempted by strong-smelling foods such as tuna or chicken livers. The sense of smell often starts a cat eating again. Avoid rich meats if the cat is vomiting or has diarrhea.

The veterinarian will give you instructions on any special measures to be taken and provide you with any medications necessary. Follow the instructions and dosage carefully and seek advice if the cat vomits soon after taking medication. Never exceed the dosage amount or frequency.

CONTAGIOUS DISEASES

The cat with a contagious disease should be isolated from other animals. It is essential to apply strict hygiene in every phase of nursing care of this cat. Many contagious diseases are airborne. This means you need to change outer clothing and scrub your hands thoroughly before handling other animals. Clorox or an iodine solution are good disinfectants for scrubbing your hands and arms.

The food and water dishes should be sterilized with hot, soapy water after each meal. Litter pans and bedding need to be disinfected with a nontoxic antiseptic such as bleach. Cats cannot tolerate a phenol derivative, so care must be taken when selecting a disinfectant. All soiled dressings, cat litter and wastes should be placed in plastic bags and sealed for complete disposal.

POSTOPERATIVE CATS

The most common surgical procedures performed in cats are neutering and repair of wounds. Local anesthetics are employed only for minor wound suturing. All other procedures involve a general anesthetic because a cat is prone to struggle and resist during the operation.

The length of time to regain full consciousness varies from a few minutes to several hours, depending on the type and length of anesthetic used and the general health of the cat prior to surgery. The partially conscious cat may have periods of excitability or try to move and stumble.

There is a growing trend among veterinarians to allow cats to return home the same day of surgery, as many feel a cat recovers better if it awakens fully in

The Elizabethan collar in place.

familiar surroundings. Most veterinarians do not have an all-night kennel attendant and believe the cat will have closer supervision at home.

The cat brought home before being fully awake needs to be confined for its own protection. Line the bottom of the carrier with a soft blanket or towel and keep the carrier in a warm, quiet room. Check on the cat at frequent intervals. As the cat becomes more alert, let it out of the carrier, allowing it to try to stand and walk for a few minutes. At this time offer a small amount of food and cool water.

Your veterinarian will give you a set of postoperative instructions on the care and feeding of your cat. Generally the cat needs rest and warmth for at least forty-eight hours. Do not allow children to handle it. If your cat has stitches, keep it confined to a room that is free of tempting shelves and furniture. Jumping can cause it to tear the stitches.

Until the cat is fully alert, eating and drinking well, it must be watched for signs of shock. Surgical shock is caused by the loss of body fluids or excessive tissue removal during surgery. The signs and symptoms are weak, rapid pulse; shallow, fast respiration; dilated pupils; and weakness or collapse. If these symptoms occur, seek professional help immediately.

The cat will gently lick and clean its incision, but if it tears at the sutures, use an Elizabethan collar to prevent their removal. Your vet will tell you when the cat is to return for a postoperative checkup and suture removal.

Watch closely for swelling, bleeding, discharge at the incision site, fever, listlessness, refusal to eat or a significant change in the cat's behavior. Most cats make rapid and complete recoveries from surgery, but your close supervision and observation will assist in reducing the dangers of postsurgical complications.

RESTRAINING THE CAT

When administering medicines, sometimes it is necessary to restrain the cat to protect yourself, since the cat's defenses consist of clawing and biting. Biting is a normal reaction of the sick animal, and under such circumstances even the most docile pet will claw and bite. Restraining is simple and best accomplished by the least amount of force.

The easiest method is to gently approach the cat, talking to it softly and calm it by stroking. Hold the body firmly against your side with your forearm while controlling its head with your hand.

Grip a struggling cat by the scruff of the neck with one hand while the other hand restrains the legs. Cats generally succumb to the firm touch of lifting by the back of the neck due to an inherited reflex action. A mother cat picks up her babies by the scruff of the neck with her teeth to transport them. Don't be afraid to hold too tightly and don't let go, otherwise the cat can escape or scratch the person giving the medication. A cat that reacts violently to medicating is best handled by wrapping the body and legs in a towel or blanket.

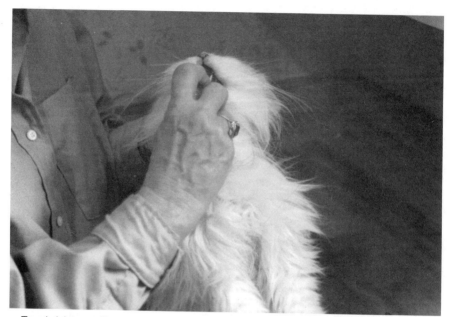

To administer a pill or capsule to a cat, gently pry its jaws apart and insert the medication at the back of its tongue.

James Curtis

After administering a pill or capsule, point the cat's head up, keep its jaws closed and stroke its throat to induce swallowing.

James Curtis

PILLING A CAT

The method used by one person alone is to sit the cat on a table facing you, holding its head in one hand while gripping the ear with your thumb and the skin at the back of the head with your fingers. Turn the head on its axis, being careful not to raise it, until the nose points upwards. Open the mouth with your other hand and drop in the pill. Close the mouth, keeping it closed until the cat swallows. A pill gun is available at most pet stores for people afraid of being bitten while placing a tablet in the cat's mouth.

EYE AND EAR MEDICATIONS

Place the cat on a table and hold it firmly from behind. To apply eye medication, open the eyelid with the thumb and forefinger of one hand. Apply the ointment directly to the cornea. Only the ointment, not the tube, should touch the eye. Gently massage the eyelid to ensure the ointment is spread around the inside of the eye. Eyedrops may be placed in the corner of the eye or on the cornea.

Ear drops are best administered by placing the cat on its side, turning its head to the side. Drop medication down into the ear, then gently massage behind the ears to spread the medication.

FORCE-FEEDING

The technique of force-feeding is similar to the one employed for pilling a cat. Use a small plastic spoon so the cat doesn't damage its teeth on metal if it bites down on the spoon. Slowly pour a small amount of liquid as far back in the cat's mouth as possible. The slower you pour, the less chance there will be of the cat choking and gagging. A small (3 cc.) plastic syringe without the needle is good because the amount of liquid can be controlled better. Often a sick cat is willing to lap at the liquid from the syringe when it's placed at the outside edge of the teeth.

Sometimes a cat may be tempted to eat by simply rubbing a tiny bit of flavored meat or food on the tip of its nose. A cat has the instinct to lick anything off its nose. Once the cat gets the taste of the meat from its nose, it may begin to eat.

FIRST AID AND THE INJURED CAT

The natural curiosity of the cat is responsible for many feline deaths and injuries. Most cat owners will have to deal with an accident or emergency at some time, particularly if the cat is allowed outside.

Eye drops are gently administered after slightly pulling out the lower lid. Any eye condition should be seen by a veterinarian first and the proper medication prescribed by him. *James Curtis*

The most efficient way of administering liquid medication to a cat is with a small, disposable syringe. *James Curtis*

Some cat owners find it easier to wrap pills in a treat their pets like. Will the subterfuge
work on this Persian patient? *James Curtis*

Success! *James Curtis*

A cat that is frightened or in pain is generally very uncooperative and must be approached and handled carefully. The cat has a habit of hiding when sick or injured, which means the animal may be difficult to find. When dealing with an injured animal, it is best to have two people present.

It is most important to transport the cat to a vet as safely and quickly as possible. Only undertake the treatment if life-threatening conditions such as stoppage of breathing, cardiac arrest, severe bleeding and shock. Some first-aid measures such as cardiac massage and artificial respiration should be undertaken only if you are out of reach of prompt veterinary help and it is a matter of life and death. Never delay obtaining professional help while you apply first aid.

Approach an injured cat with caution. Have a towel or blanket ready to wrap around the cat. This serves as a restraint and assist in lifting to prevent further injury. Soothe the animal by talking quietly and calmly.

If there is a possibility of internal injuries or fractures, approach the cat from behind. Lift the cat gently by placing one hand on the scruff of the neck and slide the other under the rump. Avoid twisting or turning the body as you lay it on a towel or newspapers in a box or carrier. If the animal is struggling, cover it with a cloth before picking it up.

Shock usually occurs following trauma and results from the collapse of the circulatory system, causing a decrease in blood pressure. In the event of shock, immediate first aid must be given.

Transport the cat as rapidly as is safely possible to a veterinarian. Keep the cat warm and comfortable. Do not administer fluids or food. Lowering the head slightly will help maintain a blood flow to the brain.

Road Accidents

When a cat has been struck by a car, the first priority is moving it to safety. Use a blanket or canvas to immobilize and cover the cat as you quickly assess the animal's condition. If the cat is breathing but immobile, then it could be suffering from a head injury or serious internal injury. Abnormal respiration and pale tongue and gums may be indicative of shock, internal bleeding or a crushed chest. These injuries need prompt medical attention.

Trapped Cats

Cats giving the appearance of being trapped in a tree are not common. Being trapped in a tree rarely results in actual injury to the cat, and it can usually come down on its own. Unless the cat is injured, rescuing it from a tree is seldom justified. To coax the cat down, place strongly flavored food at the base of the tree. Walk away and leave the cat alone.

A cat trapped in a drainage or ventilation duct and physically unable to move can become panic-stricken, therefore extremely difficult to handle. It may be necessary for a vet to sedate the cat before attempting extrication.

The proper way to pick up a struggling cat.

Burns

Chemical Burns These are caused by caustic acids and alkalis and resemble a scald. The wound is moist and oozing, with the skin around the burned area usually sloughing off. It may be several hours to days before visible injury is seen. To treat, flush the contaminated area with copious amounts of cold water to remove any chemical residue. Apply diluted bicarbonate of soda for acid burns and vinegar for alkali burns.

Electrical Burns An animal's body is an excellent conductor of electricity. The shock of 110 volts of electricity may kill a cat. This type of burn is particularly common with kittens. The young cat will bite through an electrical wire, causing severe burns of the mouth and tongue. Shock and often cardiac arrest will follow.

Before touching the cat, make sure the current is turned off. If breathing and heartbeat have stopped, CPR may need to be started by you, unless you can obtain veterinary help within five minutes. Always treat for shock and seek prompt medical help. Electrical burns generally cause deep tissue damage and are slow to heal.

Heat Burns Burns from hot water or cooking fats are more common than a dry burn. Cats have an innate distrust of objects such as a hot iron, but their affinity for warmth can lead them to stoves and fires.

Soak the affected area with cold water immediately to reduce tissue damage. Apply a cold, wet compress dressing to the burn, then seek professional help. For extensive burns, treatment for shock will probably be needed.

Drowning

Cats notoriously dislike water but are able to swim. They are unlikely to drown unless the water is rough or they are unable to reach safety to climb out. If you rescue a cat that appears to have drowned, hold it upside down, suspended by the hind legs, and swing it to and fro vigorously. This will remove excess fluid from the lungs while acting as a stimulant to commence breathing. In some cases artificial respiration and/or cardiac massage may be needed.

Dislocations

Dislocations occur when a bone has slipped from a joint and is usually rigid. There will be pain and swelling around the joint and the leg may point in an odd direction. If a dislocation is suspected, immobilize the cat, treat for shock, then seek professional help.

Fractures

This is the most common bone injury and may be readily observed by the layman. The causes of fractures are numerous and varied. The greatest number of fractures are caused by automobile accidents.

The two main objectives when rendering first aid are guarding against further injury and reducing pain. A simple fracture can be turned into a compound fracture by allowing the cat complete freedom of movement or careless handling on the part of the person administering first aid treatment. Always treat for shock.

Fractures of the lower parts of the limbs are the most common. The animal is unable to put its foot on the ground and hobbles along with the injured limb swinging freely.

If you suspect a limb fracture, lay the cat on its side with the injured leg facing up. To splint the injured leg, place it on a small piece of wood or cardboard. Wrap the leg and splint securely with bandage or cloth strips.

If the cat has sustained a pelvic fracture, it will be unable to support any weight on its hind legs. This fracture does not require splinting. Keep the cat warm, quiet and in a confined space, treat for shock, then see your veterinarian.

Frostbite

Exposure to extreme cold causes destruction of the tissue. Circulation in the nose, toes, feet, tips of ears and tail are affected.

The frostbitten skin becomes cold and white, with loss of hair in mild cases. In severe cases there is a loss of hair followed by redness and pain. The affected area will swell, then shrivel. The skin sloughs away, leaving an open, weeping surface.

If the frostbite is mild, increase circulation to the area by rubbing with your hand. Seek professional veterinary help for all cases.

Heat Exposure

Heat stroke is less common in cats than in dogs. The cat can withstand greater extremes of temperature. In hot weather, however, the cat can readily succumb to heat stroke if confined in a closed car or house with no ventilation. Improperly ventilated carriers are a common cause of heat stroke.

The signs and symptoms of heat stroke are panting, vomiting and the appearance of general shock. Rapid action is needed to reduce the body temperature. Give the cat cool water to drink immediately. Lower the body temperature by sponging the cat with cold water or wrapping it in cold wet towels. Apply ice packs to the body, particularly to the head and chest. Transport it immediately to a veterinarian, as the cat is going to need fluid and electrolyte replacement given intravenously.

Poisoning

Cats are very seldom deliberately poisoned. The habit of licking paws and fur causes most feline poisoning. The cat has a poor ability to neutralize and excrete poisons, making relatively harmless substances toxic to them.

Ensure that your cat has proper ventilation when left alone.

James Curtis

Household chemicals and cleaners are the greatest hazards to cats. Pesticides, cleaning compounds, human medications, paints, cosmetics and many household plants can be fatal to the cat. The feline has a particular sensitivity to petrochemicals, coal-tar products and their related substances. Common Tylenol (acetaminophen) is lethal to the cat, and while not as toxic as Tylenol, aspirin should not be given to a cat unless directed by a veterinarian.

Poisoning requires prompt veterinary assistance. Many poisons cause the same symptoms. Call your veterinarian first to find out if you should induce vomiting before bringing the animal in for treatment. If possible take the poison or its container with you.

The signs and symptoms of poisoning are vomiting, pain, diarrhea, trembling, convulsions, panting, slimy mouth, telltale breath odor, burns on mouth or coma. Any of these may also be symptoms of other problems.

First aid measures are limited unless you know the type of poison. Emetics can help reduce absorption of the poison by the stomach if given within thirty minutes. Vomiting must never be induced in an unconscious animal, in cases of phosphorous, corrosives or certain volatile materials. If in doubt, do not induce vomiting. All poisons cause shock, which must be treated while getting the cat to veterinary help.

One of the factors contributing to indoor cats outliving those cats that are allowed outside is limited exposure to poisonous plants. Many common plants are harmful to cats, and the amount ingested determines the severity of the reaction.

Plant poisoning usually causes a severe digestive upset, accompanied by drooling, depression and lack of appetite. Some plant poisons affect the central nervous system, causing poor coordination when walking to sudden paralysis, convulsions and death.

Seek prompt medical attention and present the plant for identification.

Table II: Common Toxic Plants

Amaryllis	English ivy	Narcissus
Azalea	Foxglove	Oleander
Bittersweet	Holly	Philodendron
Boxwood	Hydrangea	Poinsettia
Chokecherry	Jerusalem cherry	Privet
Crown of thorns	Lantana	Rhododendron
Daffodil	Larkspur	Swedish ivy
Daphne	Laurel	Wandering jew
Delphinium	Lily-of-the-valley	Wisteria
Dumb cane	Lupine	Yew
Elephant's ear	Mistletoe	

WOUNDS AND BITES

A wound is any break in the body surface. This may take the form of a simple cut or incised wound that bleeds freely. A laceration is a jagged, irregular tear that bleeds little. A puncture caused by a bite will generally become infected. A contused wound is one that may take the form of any of the three types of wounds but is accompanied by bruising of the surrounding tissue.

It is important to determine the type of bite you are treating. The bite from another cat, a dog or a rodent can generally be determined by the number of teeth marks, the distance between the marks and their size.

The first priority of any wound is to stop bleeding. Venous bleeding is deep red and will ooze or bleed slowly. Arterial blood is bright red and spurts. Arterial bleeding is life-threatening and must be stopped immediately. Apply direct pressure over the wound with a wad of material, tissue, clean rags or towels. If nothing is available, use your fingers directly on the wound until the bleeding ceases. Once you remove the pressure, be careful not to tear away the protective material and start the bleeding again.

In the case of minor lacerations, clean the wound with a weak solution of either table salt, baking soda or hydrogen peroxide. Shave the hair around the wound and fill with an antimicrobial cream.

A cat or rodent bite is often a puncture wound and seldom visible when it happens. These bites need careful watching, as cats are prone to infections that manifest themselves in abscesses. It may take three or four days for the abscess to form. One of the major causes of abscesses is the induction of hair into the wound by the adversary's teeth. Attempt to pluck the hair tufts from the puncture wound in order to prevent abscess formation.

It is best to let your vet lance and drain the abscess rather than allow it to burst on its own. Antibiotic therapy along with regular cleaning of the wound is needed in either case.

Venomous Bites and Stings

First aid for a snake bite is extremely important. Prompt medical attention within an hour is needed to save the cat's life. If your vet is not available, then call your family doctor. Many doctors have saved an animal's life in an emergency.

The snake bite exhibits rapid swelling at the site of the bite. These bites are usually found on the face, neck or forelegs. There will be two fang marks.

Spider and bee stings need immediate treatment by your veterinarian. There is little you can do for them at home. Many spiders are toxic to cats, so if possible kill the spider and take it with you for identification. These bites will usually be seen on the mouth or lips. Swelling occurs in direct proportion to the amount of venom the spider injects.

The poisonous effect of bee, wasp or hornet stings may produce severe shock in cats. The treatment of choice is intravenous steroids along with other supportive measures. Get the cat to a veterinarian as quickly as possible.

8

Understanding Body Type

ONE OF THE MOST important attributes of the purebred cat is its type or body conformation, encompassing every aspect of the cat's form including size, shape, stance, proportions, tail length, shape of head, eye set and ear position. Conformation of the body can also be affected by diet. The potential of a cat can be thwarted by poor nutrition, but a good diet cannot alter a poor body type into that of a grand champion.

Genetic differences of conformation are generally divided into two main categories. By examining the conformation in the different cat breeds we see a general unity of feline form. However, each breed has a type that makes that breed unique.

To understand what breeds may be in the ancestry of random or mixed-bred cats or those with parentage unknown, we must have a basic knowledge of body and head type. I have based this study of body type on the individual breed standards used in show standard guidelines.

NATURAL BREEDS

Abyssinian

This popular breed has a medium-long body that is lithe and graceful. Despite the dainty look, it shows a well-developed, muscular strength without coarseness, striking a medium between the extreme body types. The legs and feet

The Abyssinian has a lithe and graceful body. *Larry Johnson*

are proportionately fine boned and slim. Small paws are oval and compact. The cat stands well off the ground, creating an impression of being on tiptoe. The long tail is thick at the base and tapers to the point.

The head is a modified, slightly rounded wedge, and profile lines show a gentle contour without flat planes. The muzzle is neither pointed nor square. The large ears are moderately pointed and are broad and cupped at the base. The large eyes are almond shaped and accentuated by a fine dark line that is encircled by a light-colored area.

American Shorthair

The body is solidly built, powerful and muscular, with well-developed shoulders, chest and hindquarters. The broad back is straight and level, but viewed from the side there is a slight slope down from the hip bone to the base of the tail. The medium-length legs are heavily muscled, straight and parallel. The firm paws are full and rounded, with heavy pads. Its medium-long tail is heavy at the base and tapers to an abrupt, blunt end.

The head is large with a full-cheeked face, giving the impression of an oblong just slightly larger than wide. The face has a sweet, open expression. The muzzle is square in shape, with definite jowls seen in mature males. The forehead forms a smooth, moderately flowing curve over the top of the head to the neck. There is no dome between the ears when the cat is viewed from the front. The chin forms a perpendicular line with the upper lip.

The medium-sized ears are slightly rounded at the tips and not unduly open at the base. The large eyes are wide, with the upper lid shaped like half an almond cut lengthwise and the lower lid shaped in a fully rounded curve. The outer corners are set slightly higher than the inner corners.

Egyptian Mau

This unusual cat has a graceful, medium-long body showing a developed muscular strength. A loose skin flap extends from the flank to the knee. The legs and feet are in proportion to the body with hind legs longer, giving the appearance of being on tiptoe when standing upright. The small, dainty feet are oval, almost round in shape. The tail is medium in length, thick at the base with a slight taper.

The head is a slightly rounded wedge without flat planes, showing a gentle contour with a slight rise from the bridge of the nose to the forehead. When viewed from the front, the length of the nose is even with its width. The muzzle is not pointed or sharp.

The ears are medium to large and moderately pointed, continuing to accent the planes of the head. They are broad at the base and set with ample width between the ears. The almond-shaped eyes are large and alert. They slant slightly toward the ears.

The American Shorthair.

Larry Johnson

Japanese Bobtail

This elegant, medium-sized cat has a long, lean torso but is not tubular, and has well developed musculature without coarseness. The long legs are slender and the hind legs are noticeably longer than the forelegs. They are deeply angulated, with the paws oval in shape. The tail is clearly visible and is composed of curves, angles and kinks. The farthest extension of the tail bone from the body is three inches.

The head appears long and finely chiseled, forming an almost perfect equilateral triangle with gentle curving lines. The cheekbones are set high. The Japanese Bobtail has a noticeable whisker break. The nose is long and well defined, and there is a gentle dip at or just below the eye level. The muzzle is fairly broad and rounds into the whisker break, and it is neither blunt nor pointed.

The large, upright ears are expressive and set wide apart, at right angles to the head rather than flaring outward. In repose they give the impression of being tilted forward. The large eyes are oval and set into the skull at a rather pronounced slant when seen in profile.

Maine Coon Cat

The muscular body of this well-liked American breed is medium to large with a broad chest. The body is long with all parts in proportion, to create a well-balanced rectangular appearance. The medium-length legs are set wide apart and proportionate to the body. The large paws are rounded and well tufted. The long tail is wide at the base and tapering.

The head is medium in width and length, giving the appearance of a squareness to the muzzle. The cheekbones are high, with a firm chin that is in line with the nose and upper lip.

The ears are large and well tufted. They are wide at the base and appear to taper to a point. The large eyes are expressive and wide set. They are slightly oblique and slant toward the outer base of the ears.

Manx

This breed shows a solid, compact body that is muscular and medium in size, with sturdy bone structure. The cat is stout in appearance, with well-sprung ribs and a broad chest. The flank has greater depth than other breeds, giving considerable depth to the body when seen from the side. The short forelegs are set well apart. The hind legs are longer, with heavy, muscular thighs. The rump is higher than the shoulders. The paws are round. The best examples are completely tailless.

The rounded head has prominent cheeks and a jowly appearance, being slightly longer than it is broad. The forehead is moderately rounded. It has a definite whisker break and round whisker pads. A gentle nose dip can be seen in profile. The well-developed muzzle is slightly longer than broad, with a strong chin.

The body of the Maine Coon gives a rectangular appearance. *Larry Johnson*

Persian

This cat has a large- to medium-sized cobby body, is low on leg, deep in the chest and equally massive across the shoulders and rump. The large paws are round, firm and tufted. The short legs are thick and strong. The forelegs are straight. The tail is short.

The head is round and massive, with great breadth of skull. The face is round with a correspondingly round underlying bone structure. The head is well set on a short, thick neck. The snub nose is short and broad with a deep, visible break. The small ears are round tipped, set far apart and low on the head, fitting into the head's rounded contour. The large, round eyes are brilliantly colored and give a sweet expression to the face.

Russian Blue

This is a fine-boned cat with a long, firm body. Muscular, lithe and graceful in carriage, its long legs are fine boned, with small, slightly rounded paws. The tail is long but in proportion to the body. It tapers from a moderately thick base.

The head is a smooth, medium wedge, being neither long and tapering nor short and massive. The muzzle is blunt and is part of the total wedge. The cat has no nose break or stop. The face is broad across the eyes, due to the wide eye set and thick fur. The muzzle is a smooth, flowing wedge, without prominent whisker pads. The chin is perpendicular with the end of the nose and level under the chin.

The ears are large and wide at the base. The tips are more pointed than rounded and set far apart, almost as much on the side as on the top of the head. The eyes are rounded in shape and wide set.

Siamese

Medium-size and a long, graceful, svelte body identify the Siamese. The conformation is a distinctive combination of fine bones and firm muscles. The shoulders and hips continue the same sleek lines of the tubular body. The hips are never wider than the shoulders. The legs are long and slim, with hind legs higher than front legs and in good proportion to the body. The small, dainty paws are oval in shape. The tail is long and thin, tapering to a fine point at the end.

The head is a long, tapering wedge, medium in size. The wedge begins at the nose, flaring out in straight lines to the tips of the ears to form a triangle, with no break at the whiskers. The long nose is a continuation of the forehead, with no break or stop.

The ears are strikingly large and pointed, set wide at the base and continuing the lines of the wedge. The eyes are almond shaped and medium in size. They slant toward the nose in harmony with the lines of the wedge-shaped head and ears.

The Persian has a cobby body.

Larry Johnson

Turkish Angora

This medium-sized breed has a fine-boned, graceful torso and is long and lithe. The rump is slightly higher than the front. The legs are long with the hind legs longer than the front. The small, round, dainty paws have tufts between the toes. The long, tapering tail is wide at the base, narrowing at the end.

The small- to medium-sized head has a wedge shape that is wide at the top with a definite taper toward the chin. The nose has a gentle slope, with no break. The chin is gently rounded, with a tapered jaw. The neck is slim and graceful.

The ears are wide at the base. They are long and pointed, with tufts on the inside, set high on the head and erect. The large eyes are almond shaped with a slight upward slant.

ESTABLISHED BREEDS

Birman

The strongly built body is elongated and stocky and carried low over the legs. The medium-length legs are heavy, with large, round paws. The tail is of medium length.

The skull is broad and rounded. The cheeks are full, with a somewhat rounded muzzle. The chin is strong and well developed, with the lower jaw forming a perpendicular line with the upper lip. The forehead slopes back and is slightly convex. The medium-length nose is Roman shaped and starts just below the eyes.

Medium-length ears are almost as wide at the base as they are tall and are modified to a rounded point at the tip. The round eyes have a sweet expression. They are set well apart, with the outer corners tilted very slightly upward.

British Shorthair

A compact cat that is well balanced and powerful, has a broad chest and level back. The neck is short, giving the cat a bull-like appearance. The shoulders are broad and flat. The short- to medium-length legs are strong and well boned. The paws are round and firm. The tail is thick at the base, tapering slightly to a rounded tip and medium in length.

The head is round and massive and well set on a short, thick neck. The forehead is rounded, with a slight, flat plane on the top of the head. There is no slope to the forehead. The muzzle is well developed, with a definite stop beyond the large, round whisker pads. The chin is firm and well developed. The nose is broad, with a gentle dip.

The medium-sized ears are broad at the base and rounded at the tips, set far apart. The large, round eyes are well open.

The head of the Siamese is a long, tapering wedge forming a triangle between the ears and nose.

Larry Johnson

The Turkish Angora has a definite taper to its gently rounded chin. *Larry Johnson*

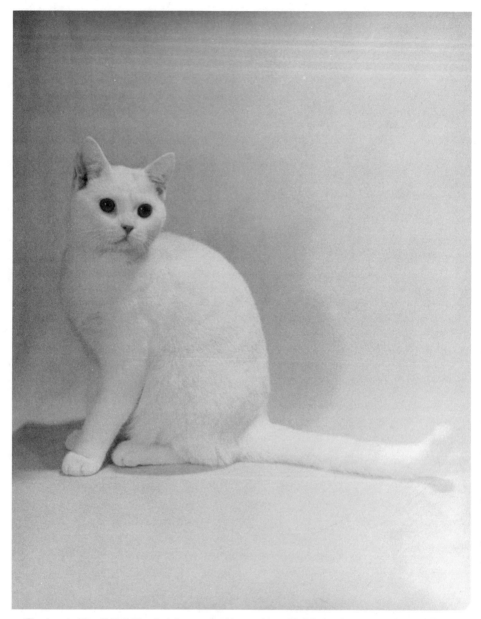

The head of the British Shorthair is round and massive, with full cheeks. *Larry Johnson*

Burmese

This breed has a medium-sized compact body with substantial bone structure. It is noted for its good muscle development and surprising weight for its size and has an ample, rounded chest. The back is level from the shoulder to the tail. The legs are in proportion to the body, with round paws. The straight tail is medium in length.

The head is pleasingly rounded. When seen from the front or side there are no flat planes. The face is full, with considerable breadth between the eyes that blends gently into a broad, well-developed, short muzzle, which maintains the rounded contours of the head. There is a visible nose break.

The medium ears, set well apart, are broad at the base and rounded at the tips. They tilt slightly forward. The large, round eyes are set well apart.

9

Coat Types and Color Patterns

$\mathbf{T}$HE LONG-HAIRED and short-haired breeds form two natural recognizable categories just as they can be divided into two major groups of body conformation. The wild or basic type of cat is the shorthair. Long hair in cats is due to a recessive gene mutation. With the exception of the rexes, wire-hair and hairless cats, all other breeds fall into one of these groups.

SHORT-HAIRED BREEDS

Abyssinian

The coat is soft and silky. It is fine in texture but dense and resilient to the touch, with a lustrous sheen. The hairs are medium in length but long enough to accommodate two or three bands of ticking. Each hair has a light section at the root and a darker section at the tip. The coat colors are red, ruddy and blue.

American Shorthair

This cat has a short, thick coat that is even and hard in texture. The coat is resilient enough to withstand cold, dampness, wounds and contact with thorny vegetation. During the winter months the fur will thicken but not become woolly. The cat can be seen in an endless variety of coat and color patterns.

The American Shorthair has a short, thick coat that is resilient. *Larry Johnson*

British Shorthair

Like that of its American Shorthair counterpart, the coat of this breed is resilient and firm to the touch. It is very dense and short. It is a full-bodied coat that exists officially in seventeen colors.

Burmese

The coat is silky and fine. It has a glossy, satinlike texture that often appears to be black rather than the actual color of dark sable brown. It is a short coat that is very close lying and thick.

Egyptian Mau

The hair is medium in length, with a lustrous sheen. The smoke-colored cat has a coat that is silky and fine textured. In the silver and bronze colors, the coat is dense and resilient in texture, accommodating two or more bands of ticking that are separated by lighter bands.

Japanese Bobtail

This cat has a medium-length coat that is soft and silky but strong, with no visible undercoat. It is a relatively nonshedding coat. The cat can be found in endless colors and patterns.

Manx

The coat is a double coat. The hair is light and soft, similar to that of a rabbit. It is dense, having a well-padded quality because of the longer, open outer coat and the close, cottony undercoat. The outer hairs are somewhat hard in texture and are glossy. This cat may be seen in all color combinations except the colorpoint formats.

Russian Blue

The cat has a short, dense coat that is thick and perfectly uniform. The plush double coat stands out from the body because of the coat's density. The undercoat gives a silvery luster of mink that is the distinctive character of the breed. The blue-gray color of the coat gives the cat its name.

Siamese

This is a short, fine-textured coat that is very close lying. It is thick and glossy. The breed is most noted for its colorpoints and its deep, vivid blue eyes.

The Maine Coon has a long, shaggy coat.

LONG-HAIRED BREEDS

Birman

The coat is medium length to long, with a silky texture, and is fairly thick on the neck and tail. This cat has a heavy collar or neck ruff. The hair on the stomach is wavy or slightly curly. The hair on the muzzle is short but thickens on the cheeks. The coat never mats because of its texture. The cat is noted for the white gloves on all four feet and is a colorpoint.

Maine Coon Cat

The hair is heavy and shaggy. It is short on the head and begins to lengthen on the withers. It thickens greatly on the body and tail. The hair is soft and silky but it is not as luxurious as the coat of the Persian. The cat has a dense frontal ruff. There are endless colors and coat patterns in this breed.

Persian

This coat is abundant and thick. It is resilient and loose-fitting to the body and denser on the neck and shoulders. The cat is noted for its lionlike mane, which continues in a deep frill between the legs. It is a fine textured, silky coat that is full of life. The cat has long ear tufts and toe tufts, and can be seen in many colors as well as tabby patterns.

Turkish Angora

The body hair is medium in length, with the hair on the ruff longer. The coat is fine, soft and silky, with a sheen. The cat has thick fur on the neck, stomach and tail. There is no undercoat. In warmer weather the coat sheds a great deal and often gives the appearance of being a short-haired coat. There are several colors in this breed.

THE BASICS OF COAT COLOR

Many important genes of cats are concerned with coat color and quality. The development of coat color has inspired a large portion of modern selective breeding in cats. Today, the infinite variety of color and markings and perfection of coat has led to the development of cats of a beauty undreamed of just a few decades ago.

The Solid Coat Colors

A solid-colored cat is the same, single color throughout. There is no shading or marking or any other variation of color or pattern in the coat. These are known as self-colored cats.

The Persian is noted for its lionlike mane.

The black is the best-known of the unicolored variety. This color is seen in both short and long coats of all body types. The dilute gene on black results in the various shades of gray, properly called blue by cat breeders; the soft shades of grey are known as lilac.

The self-colored blue cat has occurred from time to time throughout the world. The beauty of this color has led to the sanctification of some of these self blues as separate breeds. These include the Korat, Russian Blue and Chartreux—examples of cats with identical color genotype. They are recognized as distinct breeds because of their history and origins. It is only the body type that distinguishes them.

All solids vary in shade to some degree, but it is difficult for the human eye to register the subtle variations of black as much as the other colors. These variations are, for the most part, due to a modifying gene known as the darkening/lightening group. The existence of these genes means that different shades of brown, blue or lilac can be selected and stabilized by selective breeding.

A solid white cat is due to a dominant white gene, but behind the solid white cat there may be literally any color, including tabby. This is because the white gene masks the expression of all other color genes. The only way the underlying genotype of an unknown white cat can be discovered is by test crossing with a colored cat. The appearance of nonwhite offspring could provide clues.

Even though the white gene is usually dominant, it does occasionally vary somewhat in its masking ability. This can be seen in a young white kitten with color spotting that disappears when the adult coat is grown. Another example is the variation in eye color and variable occurrence of deafness. Most white cats have copper, blue or odd-color eyes. This is caused by variable removal of pigment from the irises. In the white cat, eye colors do not appear to breed true.

Deafness, which is more commonly associated with blue-eyed whites, may affect one or both ears. This is due to a degeneration of the cochlea and is irreversible. This deafness commonly begins four to six days after birth.

Patterns, Shaded and Tipped Coats

Tabby and Spotted Patterns   The tabby cat is the wild or basic type from which all others evolved. There are four patterns in tabbies. There is the mackerel, which is the tiger-striped that is the best known of all tabby patterns. The blotched or classic pattern is the true wild type and is the pattern that was derived from the wild feline ancestors of the domestic cat. The Abyssinian is the third pattern. The spotted pattern is generally considered to be a tabby.

A *mackerel pattern* has stripes that are clearly set off. A straight dark line runs down the back from the head to the base of the cat's tail. Dark stripes branch off from this main strip and run down the sides. The legs have stripes. The tail has even rings of striping, with a dark tip. There are two rows of dark dots on the stomach. The forehead has a dark marking that looks like the letter M starting

An example of the blotched
or classic tabby pattern.
Larry Johnson

An example of the mackerel tabby pattern.   *Larry Johnson*

over the nose and between the eyes. There are several dark pencil lines running to the ears. The chest has two bands that resemble a necklace.

The *blotched pattern* is also known as the *classic pattern* and comes closest to the marking seen in wild cats. The main difference between this pattern and the mackerel pattern is the unmistakable dark patches on the cat's shoulders and sides. These patches are rimmed by one or more lines. The head, legs, tail and stomach markings are the same in the blotched pattern as in the mackerel pattern.

The *spotted pattern* has dark dots that are either round or oval in shape all over the body and legs. These dots are clearly set off from each other. This type of pattern can be clearly seen in the leopard coat. The shape of the dots are generally uniform. The legs have stripes and the forehead bears the M mark. There is a narrow stripe running down the back.

The *Abyssinian pattern* is almost devoid of markings on the body. Except for the underbelly, all the hairs are banded. The underbelly hair is light and single colored. The pattern has dark patches, stripes or marking only on the forelegs, low on the flanks and on the tail.

Tabby Colors

The basic tabby is genetically black, having the same color genes as the self black. Breeders work to produce a rich brown underlying coat instead of the drab gray. They have also tried to produce a deep orange or yellow in pure breeds that is far removed from the ginger color seen in most random-bred cats.

Brown and red are the best known colors in tabbies, but the tabby markings can be found in any of the basic colors of the self blues, chocolates, cinnamon, lilac and cream. All the color variations found in the mackerel, blotched and spotted patterns can be found in the Abyssinian.

The Shaded and Tipped Colors

The shaded or tipped coat is one of the most striking in long-haired cats. The better-known of the shaded colors are in the silver group. All shaded or tipped coats share a common characteristic of colored tips on the hairs, as well as overlying a pale undercolor. Black is the best-known variety of tipping, but it can be seen in blue due to the dilute gene, in chocolate due to the brown gene and in lilac because of a combination of these genes. The difference from a shaded is the degree of tipping. The smokes have the greatest amount, while the chinchilla has the least amount of tipping.

The chinchilla silver has a coat of light-silver white. There is an even sprinkling of black tipping over the head, back, flanks and topside of the tail. This light tipping gives the appearance of a light frosted look. The remainder of the coat is a characteristic brilliant, sparkling white.

The shaded silver coat is abundantly tipped, giving the appearance of a colored mantle. The coat looks as if it has been brushed with molten silver across the head, back, flanks, outside of the legs and top of the tail. The tipping is

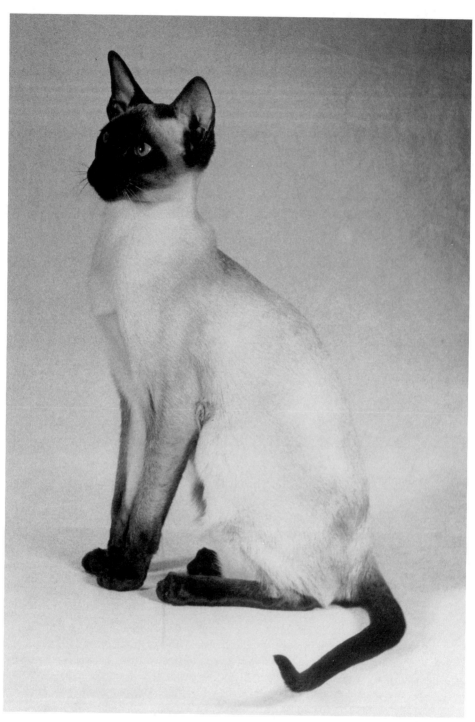

Colorpoint is caused by a gene that is part of the albino series of alleles.　　*Larry Johnson*

darker in the shaded than in the chinchilla, as the pigment is deeper down the hair shaft.

The color variations above are more commonly seen in smokes. The greater degree of pigmentation shows up more clearly in the smoke. The best known smoke color is black. The smoke cat lying down can be almost indistinguishable from a solid colored animal until it stands and displays the contrasting white undercoat.

The cameo is the red equivalent of the silvers. This color phase has an almost white undercolor, with an overlay of rich apricot to red tipping.

There are three varieties of cameos corresponding to the three degrees of tipping. The shell cameo is the palest, with a near-white undercolor and a delicate light red tipping. This would be a red chinchilla. The shaded cameo or shaded red has a near-white undercolor but a much darker red tipping and overall appearance. The darkest is the smoke cameo, which has a light cream or off-white undercolor. The red smoke, as the smoke cameo is sometimes called, has a veiling of deep, even red.

Colorpoints

In thinking of a cat with colorpoints, most people think only of the Siamese. Genetically, the Siamese is a pattern not a breed, as colorpoints are a pattern.

A cat with pale-colored hair on the body and darker hair on the nose, ears, feet and tail and blue eyes is known as a color-pointed cat. The first breed to be developed with colorpoints was the Siamese.

The colorpoint is caused by a gene that progressively diminishes the amount of pigment in the hair and eyes. There is little pigment in the body hairs and more at the points. This is due to the difference in skin temperature, being lower at the points. Production of pigment depends on temperature. The lower the temperature, the more pigment will be produced.

All the solid, tabby and tortoiseshell colors can occur in the colorpoints. Probably the best known of the colors are dark seal brown, chocolate and lilac. The red and cream are attractive points, with the coloring being particularly delicate in the cream.

The eyes of these Siamese-patterned cats show a distinctive shade of clear, brilliant blue in the iris that results from partial depigmentation in the eye. One side effect of the Siamese gene is that it can cause abnormalities in the optic nerves, resulting in a faulty connection between the eye and brain. Many color-pointed cats have reduced binocular or three-dimensional vision.

Multiple Color Patterns

The Tortoiseshell This is a patchwork pattern of two color variations found in a random mixture. The orange and black is the most prevalent pattern. The normal range of color variations can be found in the solids. The tortie pattern

Tortoiseshell is a patchwork pattern of two color variations found in random mixture.

Larry Johnson

The calico is a tortoiseshell and white.

Larry Johnson

can be found in a dilute, such as the blue-cream and lilac-cream, and also in the tabby pattern.

One of the features of the tortoiseshell is the large variation in color and patterning that can be found. Genetically the difference is minor, for these variations are caused mainly by random selection.

Piebald Spotting Piebald or white spotting is caused by a dominant gene with a variable expression. The amount of white varies, depending on whether the cat has one or two of these genes. This spotting can range from gloves on the feet, a nose smudge to white over most of the body. The most common are the self-colors and white. The tortoiseshell and white is commonly known as *calico*.

EYE COLOR

One of the most outstanding and remarkable features of the cat is the wide variation of eye color. Eye color is inherited independently of coat color. Eye color actually refers to the color of the iris.

Eye color can range from rich shades of copper to pale shades of yellow or shades from deep emerald green to brilliant blue. The brown and dilute genes do influence pigmentation of eye color, but availability of polygenes and chance can override the effect of these major genes.

The most prevalent eye colors are copper, yellow, hazel, green-blue (as in the dominant white) and blue (as in the Siamese).

10

Clues to Parentage

BY COMPILING THE INFORMATION on types, it is often possible to solve the riddle of parentage. Sometimes the process is simple, as a cat will be an obvious purebred. Other times it is more difficult to determine what breeds are in the background of a given random-bred. Occasionally it can be almost impossible to define any particular breed behind the random-bred cat.

Having an idea of what breeds make up the ancestry of the cat with parentage unknown gives you a better understanding of your cat's personality and some insight into why your cat could behave and react the way it does.

BODY AND HEAD TYPES

The following illustrations of body type show an example of four of the basic body types seen in the natural breeds.

A cobby body, low on leg, with a deep chest and level back. The short, compact body is typical to the Persian.

A solid, muscular body, medium in length, that is slightly longer than it is tall. This is seen in the American Shorthair.

This is a long, svelte body with long
legs. The structure is fine. This is
the tubular body of the Siamese.

The large body appears to create a
well-balanced, rectangular appearance with a broad chest and wide-
set legs. This long body is seen in
the Maine Coon Cat.

The following illustrations are head types of four of the most popular natural cat breeds.

The Persian
The round, massive head has great breadth of skull. The short, snub nose has a visible break. Full cheeks, small ears, set far apart, with large, round eyes.

The Siamese
A long, tapering wedge, starting at the nose, flaring out in straight lines to the ear tips forms a triangle. Almond-shaped eyes slant to a long, straight nose with no break.

The Maine Coon Cat
Medium in width and length with a squareness of the muzzle. The cheekbones are high and the large ears are wide-set. The large eyes have a slightly oblique setting, slanting toward the outer base of the ear.

The American Shorthair
A large head, with full cheeks and squared muzzle giving an appearance of an oblong, slightly longer than wide. The ears are medium and the eyes large, with the outer corners slightly higher than the inner corners.

THE OBVIOUS PUREBRED

The cats in Example A appear to be Persians. On the left is Qd. Ch. Silverluv's Spun Sugar of Ashkarr, a very fine chinchilla silver Persian. The cat on the right, Miep of Hope Haven, is a rescue with parentage unknown. There is no information on Miep's background, parentage or age.

Look at the overall body structure. Both have the same type of compact, cobby body. While Miep's front legs are slightly longer, they are short and in proportion to her body.

Both have round, massive heads set on short, thick necks that are typical of the Persian breed. This is another clue to Miep's parentage. The Persian standard calls for a short, snub nose that is broad, with a visible break. Miep has a nose that is slightly longer than Spun Sugar's, but she has a visible break. Sugar and Miep have small round ears set wide apart and low on the head.

While both cats have long thick coats, Miep's coat is not as long. Due to massive matting and flea allergy, her coat was shaved down when she was rescued, a few months before this picture was taken. Both cats have the fine sprinkle of black tipping scattered on their coats.

By comparing the champion and the rescue, we can see that Miep is, in all probability, a purebred Persian.

A COLORPOINT OUTCROSS

The cat in Example B has colorpoints on the face, legs and tail, giving the first clue to its parentage. The colorpoints in a cat breed are either going to come from the Siamese or Birman. The Himalayan, Balinese, and Colorpoint Shorthairs are the result of a Siamese mated with another breed. These other breeds, while established and recognized, are not natural breeds but are manmade hybrids.

The head of the cat in Example B is a long, tapering wedge starting at the nose and flaring in straight lines to the tips of the ears to form a triangle. This same shape is seen in the Siamese. The full, round cheeks are those of the American Shorthair. This cat has a straight and level back, with the solid muscular look of the American Shorthair, but the body is long like that of a Siamese.

The short, thick coat appears to lie fairly close to the body. Siamese have fine, close-lying coats, while American Shorthairs have thick, even coats. The colorpoints came from a Siamese or Birman. The coat gives the final clue.

This cat is the product of a mating between a Siamese and either a domestic or American Shorthair. Remember the American Shorthair has its beginning from the ordinary domestic shorthair.

Example A: Qd. Ch. Silverluv's Spun Sugar of Ashkarr, left; and Miep of Hope Haven, right.

James Curtis

Example B.   *James Curtis*

KNOWN WITH UNKNOWN

Sabrina of Hope Haven in Example C is a cat with one known parent and one unknown parent. The mother, a red pedigreed Persian, is the known parent. Sabrina is the result of an unplanned mating, and from her appearance the father could be a domestic shorthair.

It is possible to see certain characteristics that Sabrina could have inherited from her mother. Her coat, not as long or full as that seen on the purebred Persian in Example D, is from a short-haired parent. The short hair is a dominant gene, while long hair is a recessive gene.

Persian ears are small, while those of an American Shorthair are medium in size. Both breeds have ears with round tips. In Sabrina the ears are medium-sized, with slightly rounded tips. The long tail is a clue to the domestic shorthair, while the fullness and length of the coat comes from the Persian.

The white gloves and laces on Sabrina's paws and the silky texture of Sabrina's coat could indicate Birman ancestry (Example E). While the Birman is noted for the gloves, these markings are seen in other breeds. The slant or tilt to the eyes is found in several breeds and is common in the domestic shorthair.

The longer face and nose on Sabrina is another indication that she is not a purebred Persian. The American Shorthair (Example F) has a medium-length nose with a gentle, concave curve from the bridge of the nose to the forehead. A combination of these two breeds can be seen in Sabrina.

Sabrina is the result of the Persian probably crossed with a domestic shorthair. It is possible but unlikely that the unknown factor was the Birman. She has more characteristics of the domestic shorthair than those of a Birman.

BICOLOR UNKNOWN

Ming, in Example G, is a rescue of unknown background. She has a compact body with substantial bone structure similar to the Burmese. She is a solid cat and like a Burmese (Example H) is deceptively heavy. She is slightly bigger than the Burmese in appearance. Ming has a medium-sized body that is closer in size to that of the larger American Shorthair.

Ming has a rounded head that is free of flat planes. Both cats have a full face, short muzzle and the same firm, rounded chins. A close look at Ming's face shows the slight, full cheek that is seen in the Shorthair. Ming also has a neck that is more like the American Shorthair. Her ears are set far apart and rounded at the tips, which is seen in both the Burmese and American Shorthair. There is one noticeable difference in Ming. Her ears are tilted slightly forward.

When an American Shorthair was mated with the Burmese, a new breed was developed. This breed was called the Bombay. The Bombay is noted for its jet-black, glossy coat and is often called the "patent leather kid with the copper penny eyes." Ming has a sleek, glossy jet-black coat with that distinctive patent leather shine. She does have a locket of white on the neck and chest.

Example C: Sabrina of
Hope Haven.
Larry Johnson

Example D: The Persian. *Larry Johnson*

Example F: The American Shorthair.
Larry Johnson

Example E: The Birman. *Larry Johnson*

143

OTHER CLUES

Occasionally the personality of a cat may give you a clue as to its heritage, as many breeds have a unique personality.

Persians are known for being sweet and gentle, rarely showing their claws. The Siamese have a reputation for being talkers and temperamental. They have a high-pitched meow that often sounds like a newborn baby crying.

The American Shorthair is a sweet-tempered cat that is outgoing and playful. This working cat is a good climber and jumper. The Burmese, the clowns of the cat world, are people oriented, with an uncanny knack for opening doors and bounding from the floor to the top of the refrigerator in one leap.

The Maine Coon Cat, a great hunter, is a kindly cat with great intelligence. The Abyssinian is lively and rambunctious, with a rather musical voice. The Egyptian Mau has a birdlike voice that is very melodious. It is a docile cat that makes friends only when it chooses.

From the description and pictures of the Bombay, Burmese, American Shorthair and Ming, you can see that it is possible for her to be considered a Bombay. My guess is that she came from a Burmese parent and a domestic shorthair parent.

She has the personality that is so unique to the Bombay. This breed is known for its wonderful intelligence and agility. It is a people-oriented cat that thrives on lots of attention. The Bombay is always the leader of the other cats and would rather spend its time supervising its humans than playing with other felines. The personality of this breed describes Ming.

MYSTERY BREED

Shalimar of Hope Haven, the white shorthair in Example I, has a mystery background. She is between two and three years of age in this picture. She is one of the mixed-breeds that appear almost impossible to really define.

Her face looks somewhat like that of the Turkish Angora's, except that her cheeks are slightly fuller and more well developed. Her body is long and fine boned, similar to that of the Siamese or Oriental Shorthair.

Her coat, while short, is very dense and plush like the British Shorthair's, yet it has a soft, silky texture. Her hazel eyes do not give us any clues to her ancestry. She is a good example of the plain domestic shorthair with probably two mixed-bred domestic shorthair parents.

A typical domestic shorthair

A typical domestic longhair

Example G: Ming of Hope Haven.
James Curtis

Example H: The Burmese. *Larry Johnson*

Example I: Shalimar of Hope Haven.

James Curtis

This information and guidance is not intended to encourage breeding but to help give you a better understanding of the companion cat. It is through understanding that we establish a better relationship with cats, having more patience and tolerance for the animal. If we know that the quiet, sweet boy is of Persian origin, for example, then we do not expect him to bound around the house like the Burmese. Have fun and enjoy solving the puzzle. Good luck with your riddle of parentage unknown.

The hunting posture.

11

Understanding the Cat

FROM THE TIME man won the cat's trust and all through the centuries since, he has puzzled over the true nature of this enigmatic animal that is both endearing and infuriating at the same time. The puzzle that is the domestic cat may never be unraveled, as the more we learn of him, the more we find there are other unexplored mysteries under that cool exterior. One thing we do know is that the cat we share our lives with is one of Nature's most successful and enduring creations.

FELINE INTELLIGENCE

Cats are extremely capable problem solvers, well able to adapt the solutions as conditions warrant. This is the feline equivalent to our insight and can be seen, for example, in the cat that opens a closet door to retrieve its favorite toy. So far, no tests have been developed to measure feline intelligence. Cats are unmoved by the work ethic and work only from desire or need. They are far more adept at living by their wits.

They have a remarkable homing ability. There are many reliable accounts of cats finding their way across hundreds of miles in order to return to familiar territories. It is thought they navigate unfamiliar terrain by responding to a combination of the earth's magnetic field and the sun.

The cat's five senses respond much more rapidly and efficiently to outside stimuli than ours do. They may or may not possess a "sixth" sense, but seem to

The cat is full of pride and decorum, rarely accepting being taught. *James Curtis*

anticipate future happenings such as an owner going on vacation or an impending storm. We wonder how they know and often puzzle over how finely attuned cats are to events around them. They can sense a pressure drop in the weather, smell rain, feel minuscule earth tremors or observe a break in your daily routine. When this happens they make provision for their future comfort.

LEARNING AND INSTINCTS

Cats readily adapt to changes in their circumstances because they remember what they have learned, then adapt experiences to new situations when presented with them.

The cat is full of pride and decorum. It rarely accepts being taught or imposed upon. Typically, the cat will avoid learning by going to any extreme. Teaching a cat cute tricks is very difficult and requires an extreme amount of patience.

The cat allows itself to be mastered to a certain extent if it sees an advantage to this. The cat learns to play games because it is responding to a delicacy or the insistence of a dominant personality. The best age for training a cat is between four and five months. Occasionally a cat will learn something on its own, such as opening a door.

Many feline behavior patterns seem to be inborn and can range from simple reflexes during nursing to the more complex and integrated sequences such as mating and maternal care.

It can be difficult to differentiate between learned and instinctive behavior. Cats are constantly modifying, altering or supplementing their behavior patterns as they observe and learn. Hunting is a good example of learned behavior.

Cats are extremely adept at learning a wide variety of behaviors without benefit of formal training, as demonstrated when your cat gets your attention by tapping on the window when it wants to be let in the house. Cats observe and deduce, then act on the information received.

The memory of a cat is not short, as people commonly tend to think. The cat is able to recognize those who treat it with love and those who mistreat it. They have a considerable sense of orientation connected to affection and loyalty.

The cat is a definite creature of habit and is resistant to any change in family, territory or routine. Try rearranging the furniture and see how quickly your cat sulks. It wants meals served at the same time every day, in the same bowl at the same place. If you suddenly change your daily routine, it will ignore you with great style for a time, showing no interest.

SLEEP BEHAVIOR

Feline insomnia is unknown, as cats spend approximately two-thirds of their lives sleeping, which is twice as much as for other mammals. Daily sleep patterns vary with weather, age, sexual arousal and degree of hunger. Kittens

Facial Expressions

Friendly Interest

Attentive

Relaxed

Warning

Ready to Attack

and elderly cats sleep more than the average adult. Warmth, security and a full stomach provoke any cat at almost any time to sleep.

Natural sleep patterns consist of numerous, short naps throughout the day. Cats with working owners tend to sleep during the day and reserve mornings and evenings as wakeful periods to socialize with their human companions. A bored cat may sleep to pass the time.

Warmth is very important to the sleeping cat. They move sleeping spots to help counteract the fall in the body temperature experienced while sleeping. This desire for warmth can present a potential danger for the cat who gets too close to a fireplace or gas stove.

Every cat has its own special sleeping spot. Generally they have a favorite spot for mornings, another for afternoons and still another for nighttime. Cats seem to prefer sleeping next to their humans at night. The reason for this seems to be the warmth of another body, companionship and security.

FELINE COMMUNICATION

Cats come in contact with their peers and humans in many ways, among them reproduction, raising kittens, defining and observing rank, defending territory and the giving or receiving of mutual warnings against dangers and enemies. This contact depends on the cat understanding the moods and intentions of other cats. It must be able to adapt its behavior to these cues, thereby influencing the behavior of other cats in return.

Cats use signs to communicate with each other. As cats do not communicate with the spoken word, these nonverbal communications play an important role as a complement to and a precursor of language with humans.

Many signs of cat language are transitory. These signs include facial expressions, sounds and gestures. Some cats may leave a more permanent sign that other cats recognize and understand even when the producer of these signs is not present.

Cat signs are meaningless if those for whom they are intended fail to observe, perceive or understand them. This giving and interpreting of sign language is innate in cats. Kittens can perform the behaviors without ever having to learn how by a certain stage of their development.

The house cat has an exceptionally vast supply of many forms of expression. Domestic cats have advanced far beyond their wild ancestors in the capacity to develop new forms of social organization and communication. It uses its body and facial expressions to communicate its intentions to all around it.

By studying the various signals that make up the cat's language, you will find that you will better understand the messages your cat is trying to convey. A basic understanding of this language will aid in deepening the bonds of friendship with your feline companion.

Whisker Communication

Friendly

Timid

Excited and Tense

FACIAL EXPRESSIONS

The extremely mobile musculature of the nose, ears, lips, cheeks and forehead can combine to create a vast variety of expressions. The rapid dilation and constriction of the pupil will give different meanings. Whiskers often accentuate the muscle movements around the foreface.

Cheek Ruff

The cheek muscles pull the cheek ruff downward and toward the throat during excitement or expectation mixed with fear. A pulsing rhythm is sometimes present. This is easy to see in cats with prominent cheek ruffs, such as those with Persian ancestry.

Ears

Ears pointed forward can convey friendly interest and different degrees of attentiveness or suspense, depending on how far up or toward the center they are pulled. Ears that are pricked up and turned slightly backward indicate a warning that an attack is contemplated. Ears that are raised and twisted back combined with hissing mean that a cat is ready to attack. Ears fully erect but furled back indicate anger.

A frightened cat lays the ears down flat. Ears that are bent back and drawn down sideways can signal a defensive attitude, fear or readiness to take flight. A cat playing or hunting will hold the ears open, erect and slightly forward.

Lips

Movements of the lips are usually combined with some type of sound. The grimace is a response to certain smells. The mouth is slightly open, with the nose and upper lip drawn upward expressing displeasure or disgust. The mouth is open very slightly and the nose is barely wrinkled.

Another lip gesture is embarrassment. The mouth may stay open or closed, with the lips drawn back and not too far upward. The nose is not wrinkled. At the same time the head will swing slowly from side to side. This gesture expresses friendly rejection to another cat approaching with friendly intentions, and translated means please be kind and leave me alone.

Pupils

Narrowed pupils may indicate aggressive threat, tension or a heightened interest. Surprise, fear and a defensive attitude are expressed by dilated pupils. Mood shifts can be magnified by changes in light, since the size of the pupils depend on light.

The Everyday Cat as the Master of Body Language

Beverly Dixon

Beverly Dixon

James Curtis

Whiskers

The position of whiskers says a great deal. When a cat is excited, tense and ready to act, the whiskers will be pointed forward and fanned out. On a calm or comfortable cat, the whiskers point outward and are less spread apart. This position can also mean a friendly disposition or indifference.

A cat that is hunting prey will thrust its whiskers forward. The shy, timid or reserved cat will bunch the whiskers together and flatten them out to the side of the face. Whiskers flat against the face signifies the cat is frightened.

Yawning

Yawning is a sign of reassurance, used to express a peaceful feeling. Seeing another cat yawn does not make a cat sleepy.

GESTURES

Gestures are body positions and movements that convey a message. The cat's ability to erect the hairs on certain parts of its body must also be included.

Aggression is expressed with erect ears, constricted pupils and tail swings in low arcs close to the body. A defensive cat crouches in a cringing position with its eyes averted and ears flat and thumps the tip of its tail on the ground. A happy cat relaxes its whiskers, perks up its ears and holds its head and tail high in the air.

Body

A stretched body can indicate that the cat is sure of itself or prepared to attack. A contracted body indicates fear. The arched back conveys the idea that the cat is in readiness for defense.

Head

A head stretched forward is ready for contact. Facial expressions and other gestures indicate whether the encounter is antagonistic or friendly. A cat feeling dominant raises its head, and inferior feelings cause the head to lower. If the head is lowered in a jerky manner and the chin pulled in or the head turned sideways, the cat is displaying a lack of interest. The cat uses this gesture if it desires not to provoke or be provoked when encountering another cat. When meeting another cat that is being very persistent, the cat that wants to avoid contact will raise its head high and pull it far back.

Legs

Stretching legs to their full length is a sign of self-confidence. Depending on the facial expression, this gesture could also mean a readiness to attack. A cat bends its hind legs to convey its uncertainty or timidity. By bending the forelegs,

Body Gestures

Happy or Relaxed

Crouched in Defense

Aggressive Stance

the cat is expressing its desire to avoid conflict, while stating it will defend itself if necessary. Complete defensiveness is communicated by bending both fore- and hind legs. A slightly raised paw indicates readiness to defend itself.

Tail

The tail is one of the best barometers of feline mood. A still, raised tail means a friendly greeting. A sudden whip of the tail shows a threat of impending attack. The highly excited cat waves its tail from side to side in jerky, rapid motions. The tip of a tail moving means slight dissatisfaction or impatience. A relaxed cat allows the tail to hang straight down. A tail held straight out behind indicates caution. The tip whips back and forth in moments of great excitement.

Hair

When the cat is afraid, the hair on its body stands erect, fairly evenly all over the body. A cat that is ready to attack or trying to threaten will raise its hair in a narrow strip along the spine and the tail. In this mood the hair will incline slightly toward the middle of both sides, forming a sharp ridge.

VOCALIZATIONS

Cats have a different vocal apparatus from humans. They can vocalize when exhaling as well as inhaling. The position of the tongue is not as important as it is in human speech. The variations in the phonetic quality of sounds are achieved mainly by changing the tension of the throat and oral muscles and by changes in the speed of air moving over the vocal cords.

There are three general sound categories in cat vocalization. Murmuring comprises the soft sounds used for acknowledgment, approval, attention, calling and greeting; purring is included in this group. The majority of these sounds are formed with the mouth closed.

The vowel sounds are another category of sound. Cats use these particular sounds, which consist of the meows, in very specific context. Most cats have an impressive vocabulary of these sounds to express needs such as hunger, grati- tude, in or out, "no," "come here," "move over," to name a few. Cats seem to train their humans more readily to this part of their language than any other.

The last group is made up of high-intensity, strained sounds. These are usually reserved for cat-to-cat communications, and consist of the hiss, spit, growl, wail and snarl. Such sounds generally indicate anger, pain or frustration. When directed at humans these sounds mean "leave me alone now."

Caterwauling

This is a song of threat and war, sometimes called wailing. It is the sound that rival tomcats emit as they approach each other. It is often mistaken by humans to be a love song between a tom and a queen.

Growling

This sound is usually accompanied by a facial expression. Growling indicates offense rather than defense. When growling, the corners of the mouth are drawn up more than the upper lip. Repeated growling will eventually turn into snarling.

Gurgling

A high-pitched gurgle means a friendly greeting. This sound is sometimes combined with gentle meows to become a chatting sound that will vary in quality in cats. It is a social contact sound. The cat has a tremendous capacity for variation on this sound. It seems to play an important role in vocal exchanges, but it has not yet been studied in depth.

The curious call the mother cat makes to her young when bringing prey is a modified version of the gurgle sound. She is telling them to come closer to look at the prey. The size of the prey determines the loudness of this call.

Hissing

This is a common warning sound. When hissing, the cat will open its mouth about halfway, drawing back the upper lips and arching the tongue. The breath is expelled with force. This is why a cat will shy away if you blow in its face. The expression of hissing without sound will succeed in repulsing a cat. Hissing is a form of expression that affects three different senses—sight, touch and hearing.

Meowing

The vowel sounds a cat makes are the meowing sounds and are used in specific context. There are several variations, such as "miaow," "meeow," "mew," and "mew wow." These sounds, which are used to demand and beg or lodge a complaint but can also mean bewilderment, form distinct words in that the cat closes its mouth after making each sound. These sounds are used in communicating with humans, and the manner in which a cat pronounces them gives the individual a specific voice.

Cats have a broad range of several types of meows. The best known of the meow sounds is that of an unhappy kitten. A short, high meow in adults expresses discontent or unhappiness. A hungry cat shows displeasure with loud, almost screaming meows. A cat seeking attention or wanting to be petted will meow softly. A form of this sound is used as a mating call between cats. This high-intensity, strained sound is usually used only between cats.

Newborn kittens do not have the full vocabulary of meow sounds the adult cat has; they can purr, growl and spit. But by the twelfth week they are able to produce most of the other adult sounds to some degree.

Purring is the vocal message of the contented cat and always a reassurance for those around it to hear.   *James Curtis*

You can learn your cat's language easily. All you must do is watch and listen.   *James Curtis*

Purring

It is thought that this sound originated as a vocalization of kittens to tell a mother they are content. When they produce this sound while nursing it does not interfere with sucking, and sound contact can be maintained with the mother cat. A mother cat purrs when approaching her kittens in order to reassure them of her presence. Older kittens purr when they are trying to get an older cat to play with them.

Adult cats purr when all is well with their world. A dominant cat will purr when approaching another cat with playful or peaceful intentions. A sick cat will purr in order to try to soothe a potential aggressor.

It is not known how cats purr. One theory maintains that it is the vibration of the false vocal cords. Another theory suggests that it is the result of turbulence in the bloodstream of the vena cava, the main vein returning to the heart.

Screeching

This sound seems to have evolved from a meowing sound and is usually used to mean distress. It is often used by a female at the conclusion of mating as a signal to the tom to move away.

Spitting

This is a warning or threatening sound. It is a sudden and violent nonvocal sound, usually accompanied by a forepaw hitting the ground. Cats use this sound as a bluff when approached by an attacker.

SCENT SIGNALS

Scent signals are often used when two cats meet. The cats touch and their scents are exchanged. Scent signals are used to mark a cat's territory.

Cats do have a body odor, which changes with the fluctuations of hormone production. Cats deposit scents through glands in their cheeks and near the anus. These scents may last for weeks. There are localized skin glands under the chin and on the pads of the feet that can secrete scent.

The exact role of these scent secretions is not very clear. We have established that cats recognize each other by the scents emitted from the cheek glands. Cats seem to spread their scent through social contacts, and certain types of physical contact seem to play a role. Cats rub against each other with the head, cheeks and flanks. They also run the length of their body under the chin of a partner or companion cat. This form of scent marking is especially noticeable in the multi-cat household. It is a means of expressing affection and friendliness for playmates. It also identifies or marks the cats that belong to that hierarchy or group.

Cats perform these same movements with other objects to spread their scent, and these scents can be recognized several days later. Notice the way your cat will rub its head or body against your leg or a piece of furniture. Cats seem to use this rubbing up against humans as a way of greeting. They recognize their own scent on the people they live with, leaving no doubt in the cat's mind who those lucky people belong to.

When cats sharpen their claws on the same object over and over again, the action serves to remove worn cuticle layers while leaving a scent. The sharpening of claws in front of other cats is a show of self-confidence. The scratch marks convey the same message.

SUMMARY

Cats use the expressions described in this chapter with varying degrees of intensity and duration. These expressions may be combined in different ways to mean different feelings and needs or create another mood. A kitten learns to use these expressions for a purpose. Cats also learn to understand the expressions of other creatures.

Much of the body language used by cats revolves around their humans. The companion cat will acquire some body signs that are reserved exclusively for this purpose, and these signals differ between cats. Individual cats develop their own particular way of getting attention. Some use predatory attacks on hands, legs, ankles or toes, while others will jump in a favorite person's lap or sit at his or her feet and talk. These quirks or idiosyncrasies are an expression of the cat's individual personality and illustrate as well the adaptability of cats in modifying their behavior to suit their environment.

Eating is one of the high points of a cat's day.

12

The Multi-Cat Household

THE DOMESTIC CAT is presumed to be an aloof creature preferring a life of solitude. This can be a misconception under some circumstances. The cat has the ability to function as a highly social animal. Most felines can lead very sociable lives, supporting each other in small groups.

Feral cats often live in groups based on a parent-offspring family unit. Cats living with people are generally very tolerant of each other, with individuals from completely different litters and backgrounds living together quite amicably.

Individual members within a group greet each other affectionately and sleep in companionable heaps. They groom each other, play together, and if threatened, the colony will defend the home territories together.

Cats in group living share many of their daily tasks. Females work as a unit to provide food for the young, nurse another mother's kittens and baby-sit. Queens share the tasks of the feeding and cleaning of newborns—often pool feeding and sharing the toilet needs of the babies.

The urge for socialization persists outside the immediate family circle. Neighborhood cats become members of a social group that meets on neutral ground. Their precise function is not understood, but it appears that membership in these feline groups helps reduce conflicts between neighbors.

In their own way, cats are social animals and do enjoy each other's company. *James Curtis*

FELINE SOCIAL HIERARCHIES

Cats develop a very complex hierarchy. This pecking order runs from the most submissive up to the most dominant individual. This structure varies with specific living arrangements. The undisputed dominant cat within its home territory may be completely deferential to cats living a short distance away. A pair of cats might amicably curl up to sleep together or groom each other, yet be totally indifferent, even intolerant, of each other when active.

The female hierarchy is rather loosely knit. Every time a queen has a litter, she advances a notch on the social scale. Females that are spayed after having litters lose some rank. Females spayed before having a heat cycle never establish a place for themselves within the social group.

The male hierarchy is different. A male is ranked according to his machismo quotient. Intact males do not escape initiation into the hierarchy. The adolescent establishes rank after several fights. Once a tom establishes his rank, he no longer has to fight unless he challenges for a higher rank, is challenged by a subordinate individual or is partaking in the initiation of a newcomer. Males are graded socially when whole. A neutered male drops in rank corresponding to the lowering of his male hormone levels. Toms altered before their initiation have, like unbred altered females, no place in the hierarchy.

TERRITORIES

Cats are very territorial. Most live alone with their human companions and are rarely visited by other cats or animals of different kinds. When an intrusion does occur, it is generally resented. This has given rise to the impression that cats are antisocial, when all they are doing is defending their territory.

Cats maintain individual territories. The social repertoire of the cat is flexible enough to allow the peaceful sharing of territories and the formation of socially integrated communities. This results in a complex net of relationships of which the average cat owner is only at best dimly aware.

A cat has its own personal home base. This can be no more than a favorite sleeping spot. Surrounding home base is the area known as the home range, encompassing the favorite places that are regularly used for eating, sleeping, grooming, playing and guarding.

The extent of home range depends upon the abundance and the reliability of the food supply, the amount of cover offered and number of cats in the neighborhood. Home range dimensions may also depend on sex, age and temperament. Females and neuters occupy small, defined spaces. Toms may command a much larger area with less defined boundaries. Toms are more tolerant of a temporary intruder than the female is.

Housebound cats have the same territorial urges as an outdoor cat. The only manifestation of this behavior you might see is an occasional defense of a favorite sleeping spot. The home range is defended by the owner; therefore the cat has no need to compete or forage for food.

The interaction of a feline family is a constant source of pleasure.   *James Curtis*

ESTABLISHING TERRITORIES

Domestic cats have a territory thrust upon them by an owner who has no knowledge of the existing feline land rights. If a newcomer is to spend any time out of doors, it will have to fight its way into the local social order and may find its yard has been incorporated into an adjacent territory. The new cat's annexation attempt may be strongly resisted. A newcomer takes its cue from its owner when marking the limits of its intended claim. Confrontation is inevitable. The fierceness of the fight depends on the age, strength and sex of both the existing holder and the newcomer. The results of these battles are final, and the change in the status is accepted without any further fighting.

DEFENDING A TERRITORY

Feral cats characteristically defend their own territory from invasion by enemies. This concept of feline territoriality remains part of the behavior pattern of today's domestic cat.

All cats use psychological "warfare" to defend their territories. Visual and vocal threats coupled with bluffs and appeasement rituals aid in keeping actual physical conflict to a minimum. When these rituals backfire, a nasty, brutish fight ensues, with one or both combatants being injured. Cat fights are short if the loser manages to escape.

Aggressive behavior is reduced in the multi-cat household when the members are altered. The house cat is much more tolerant of other cats than a feral cat would be. Regular meetings on neutral ground enable neighboring cats to get acquainted with each other. This helps prevent outbreaks of combat.

Domestic home territories are generally crowded. There is a network of paths and shared thoroughfares to meeting grounds. In a colony of domestic cats, the areas beyond the home range are complex. Fighting at every corner is not feasible, so the colony develops a highway code based on mutual avoidance. The cat about to venture forth checks the path ahead and waits for a clear route. The cat on the communal path seems to have the right of way, regardless of its rank in the social hierarchy.

Time scheduling is another avoidance technique employed by cats in social interaction. Cats possess an excellent sense of timing, and this is used to increase the efficiency of the territory. Cats sharing boundaries establish a routine whereby one has the right of way in the morning while the other has the right of way in the afternoon. One cat has an absolute uncontestable right to a sunny spot in the morning, while a second cat claims that equally uncontestable right in the afternoon.

Confrontation may be resolved through a staring routine. This is observed in two cats when they approach a crossroad. Both cats will stop and attempt to stare the other down for the right of way. One may win or both will decide to retreat to avoid a fight. Occasionally a full-scale ritual threat may develop, but

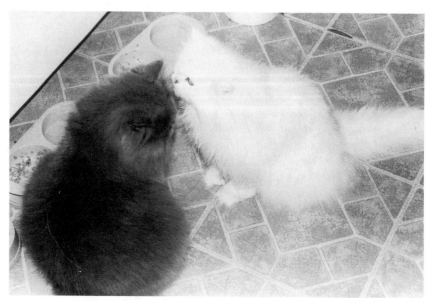

Sugar grooms Malachi after dinner. *James Curtis*

Ming challenges Miep for a sunny window
seat. *James Curtis*

this usually ends without violence. The subordinate cat runs off with the victor chasing. These minor skirmishes do not confer any type of permanent status on the winner. The next time these two cats meet, the other could be the victor. Social status is not a territorial matter.

CATS AND DOGS TOGETHER

The occurrence of two-way communication that cats have between each other as well as between unrelated species and humans is remarkable. They seem to possess the ability to learn to understand and respond to other life forms.

Cats can coexist amicably with dogs regardless of stereotypes to the contrary. The character of both the cat and dog play an important part in peaceful coexistence. Some will simply tolerate each other, while others become great friends. The sight of a dog and cat sharing a common water bowl is not uncommon. After a period of initial caution, the cat and dog may become inseparable companions.

If the dog is calm and even-tempered, the cat will slowly accept a friendship. Dogs that are nervous or high-strung are normally viewed with extreme caution by most cats. Coexistence with dogs having an unalterable hunting instinct, as with many terriers, hounds and sporting breeds, is difficult at best and is generally not recommended. On the other hand, many cats live very contentedly with dogs of these breeds. Much depends on the animals concerned.

It is better to introduce cats to a dog when they are kittens for any deep, intimate relationship to form. The adult dog tolerates kittens and cats much better than it tolerates other dogs. A female dog that has experienced motherhood often takes a kitten under her wing to raise just like she would one of her own pups.

Once peaceful coexistence has been established, the cat and dog defend each other from intrusions and engage in mutual grooming. The cat very rarely is the first to instigate an attack on the dog unless the dog gets too close to a queen with a litter of young kittens. Coexistence between species is the natural substitute for a cat deprived of normal social interaction with other cats.

INTRODUCING THE NEW CAT

Extra care and patience on the part of the owner are the prerequisites to introducing a new cat into the household of an established cat. An unplanned or badly planned meeting can result in the cats being enemies forever.

I prefer to introduce a newcomer by leaving it in the carrier and placing the carrier in the middle of the colony's favorite room. This gives the resident cats the opportunity to approach the carrier and smell the newcomer. It also affords the new cat a chance to smell the existing colony. At the same time the cats can see each other, thereby communicating with vocal sounds and body language. Generally I leave the cat in the carrier for an hour or two, depending on the reaction of the rest of the household.

Far from being bitter enemies, cats and dogs often make the best of friends. *James Curtis*

Sweet Bits naps with Sherry, her dog. *James Curtis*

When the cat is removed from the carrier it should be taken to the area where the litter trays are kept and placed in one of them. This serves two purposes: It shows the newcomer where the box is located and gives it the chance to leave its scent there along with the existing cats. Follow it while it makes the initial tour of the new home, then leave it to establish its position in the social hierarchy. With this method of introduction, I have never had a cat fight among the house cats either at the time of introducing a newcomer or later.

A newcomer may take several days to establish its rank in the pecking order or it may immediately be relegated to the bottom of the heap. Rarely can a newcomer take over the leadership position upon introduction to the group.

When introducing a new cat to an established cat, never try to force acceptance of the newcomer. Let the relationship with the established resident grow gradually. If the established cat ignores the new one, leave them alone. By allowing them to set the pace, the chances of them building a peaceful coexistence are greater.

Cats do not like to be pushed or forced into doing anything. Instead, they want to do things in their own way and in their own time. Because of this aspect of their personality, it may take time for an older cat to accept a younger one.

PROBLEMS OF MULTI-CAT HOUSEHOLDS

One of the biggest problems in a multi-cat household is preventing and controlling illness. Many viruses are highly contagious, so it is often best to isolate a sick cat and prepare to treat the rest. A new cat can cause the entire population to get sick, and conversely the established colony can cause illness in the newcomer. For this reason, it is preferable to isolate a new cat for ten to fourteen days and watch for any signs or symptoms of illness in the entire community.

Provide separate food and water dishes for each cat. Minor squabbles can quickly develop if there is only one food dish. Also, with communal feeding, the cats at the bottom of the social scale may not always get enough to eat.

Cats living together like to play together. When there is group living, make sure that each cat has its own toy. Cats share toys and play time, but they still like to have a toy that is special to them for a certain amount of solitary play.

If there is a longhair and shorthair living together, they will groom each other. It is possible for the short-haired cat to have fur balls due to the grooming of its long-haired friend. Therefore treat both with a fur-ball remedy.

Ensure that the established cat gets plenty of attention and love when introducing a new cat. This reduces the possibility of jealousy developing toward the newcomer. Each cat needs a certain amount of individual time and attention. You will find that each cat will establish its special time period with you. When that happens, do not allow another cat to interfere with that special time.

If the single cat is left alone much of the day, then it is best to adopt a second cat. Cats enjoy the company and companionship of other cats. A solitary

James Curtis

Beverly Dixon

M. Pyles

174

cat is not as happy as the cat with other felines if living in a home where the owners are at work all day. It is just as easy to care for two cats as it is to care for one, and the returns are doubled.

13

The Rescue and
Secondhand Cat

THERE ARE VAST, UNCOUNTED NUMBERS of cats born in the United States every year. Far too many end up as rescued or secondhand cats. These cats often have special needs and problems. What is a rescue or secondhand cat? Is there a difference between the two?

My definition of a rescue cat is one that has been abandoned or lost for any reason. A secondhand cat has gone to more than one so-called permanent home since the age of three months. The average kitten has two homes. The first is the birth home. From there the cat goes to its first permanent home. A cat that for any reason goes to the second or more permanent home is the secondhand cat.

In either case, these cats do not react like a loving house pet the first few nights in a new home. It may take weeks before the cat learns to trust a new owner and to offer its affection. If you can understand this and are willing to wait, then you can have a rewarding relationship with the rescued cat. If you want a cat that sits in your lap the first night and immediately purrs, do not adopt a rescued cat.

TYPES OF RESCUED CATS

Stray Cats

It is not known exactly how many stray cats there are in the United States. Some experts estimate that for every two pet cats there is one stray. A stray has

The stray generally dies from starvation.

The stray is accustomed to human companionship and often tries to adopt a new human companion.

three alternatives for survival. It can struggle on its own for a while, but generally dies from starvation, disease or accident. The cat may join a colony of feral cats, or it may try to find itself a new home. Strays that find new homes are lucky and probably in the minority.

A stray accustomed to human companionship may approach a person. The cat may be timid and dirty, but given time and care will make a wonderful companion. This does not happen overnight and requires love and patience on the part of the new owner.

Shelter Cats

These cats have been removed from secure homes for a variety of reasons. They may come from diverse backgrounds, but all have been abandoned, and often their trust in humans has been abused.

Secondhand Cats

The ideal life for a cat is to go from the birth home to a permanent home, living its entire life with the same owner. Many do not have this ideal life and for some reason are sent to another home. A change in homes produces a certain amount of stress in most cats.

Stress manifests in behavioral changes such as aggression, spraying, or food refusal for several days. A cat that changes homes does not readjust overnight. It takes time for the secondhand cat to give its love and trust to a new person. The new owner must earn its devotion and trust and these must come naturally.

CATS WITH PHYSICAL TRAUMA

The cat that has sustained injuries from physical abuse may have a combination of psychological problems. The physical injuries heal quickly, but the psychological trauma can take months to subside. There are no shortcuts to healing the cat's psyche. The key to restoring the confidence of this cat is time, love and patience.

These physical injuries may be due to either abuse inflicted by another human or sustained while struggling as a stray to stay alive. Your veterinarian can ascertain how the injuries were sustained. The cat that has been abused is going to suffer a certain amount of psychological trauma that must be dealt with over a period of time.

This cat often does not trust humans and is afraid of being hurt again; only time can teach the cat to trust. Some never recover from the fear of being hurt and will always growl or attempt to nip when touched in a sensitive area. The best way to cope with this behavior is to first understand the reasons behind it. Growling and biting are fear-induced behavior responses.

Avoid touching an obvious injury site when handling the cat. The cat may be sensitive around the injury site long after healing is complete. If it does growl, verbally reassure it that you are not going to hurt it. Never force the issue by touching the sensitive area to prove to the cat that it will not be hurt again.

To hit a cat that tries to bite only reinforces the reason for distrust. The cat is biting out of fear. Firmly tell it "no" as you give verbal assurance that you are not trying to hurt it. You may never completely teach the cat not to bite.

This cat tends to hide while its injuries are healing. If the injuries are severe, confine the cat during the recovery period to make treating and medicating easier on you both.

COPING WITH PSYCHOLOGICAL TRAUMA

The rescued or secondhand cat generally exhibits several signs of psychological trauma. These signs can be overcome in time with effort on the owner's part. It is important to understand the reasons behind the particular behavior.

The abandoned cat is stressed by the changes in its life. This cat is frightened and bewildered. Anxiety and depression may develop as a result of stress it experiences. Some may exhibit aggressive behavior from fear of strange people and surroundings.

For the past several years I have worked with rescues. While I do not claim to be an expert in feline psychology, over the years I have developed some commonsense methods and approaches to dealing with these special problems and needs, often by trial and error or simply out of necessity.

Not Eating

There is no need for alarm if a cat refuses food when placed in a strange or new environment. Remember, the cat is frightened and insecure. Give it ample love and reassurance. Show it where its food is located but do not force it to eat. Usually after twenty-four to forty-eight hours the cat will have settled down and begun eating on its own.

The cat may be accustomed to a different type of food and waiting for the same type it was accustomed to eating in another home. When it gets hungry, it will eat. Undue worry or fuss over the cat could encourage the animal to become a finicky eater. A cat is a resilient animal and can survive for several days without food. To miss a meal or two is not going to harm or endanger a healthy cat.

If the cat is very thin and suffering from malnutrition, it needs first to be seen by a veterinarian and put on a high-quality diet that includes a good vitamin supplement.

Hiding

It is common for a rescue to hide when introduced to a new home. Hiding is a response to fear and stress. The best way to treat the cat is leave it alone, allowing it to seek what it perceives to be a safe refuge within its new surroundings.

If the cat does not come out after a couple of hours, then approach the hiding area, giving soft verbal reassurances. Do not attempt to touch the cat. It may not emerge in your presence for a few hours or even a few days. As it develops confidence and recovers from stress, it will come out. When this happens, control your impulse to rush over and pick it up; instead, stay where you are, quietly encouraging it. Let the cat make the first move and come to you.

To rush or grab at a cat only frightens the animal and serves to reinforce the problem you are trying to overcome.

Growling

Newly adopted cats are often returned to shelters because they are perceived to be mean or nasty tempered. Further investigation generally reveals the insecure cat's response was a hiss, spit or growl. The new owner immediately decided the cat was mean and returned it to the shelter without giving it enough time to adjust.

The chances of a grown cat growling, hissing or spitting for the first few days in a new home are highly probable. If the cat growls when approached, back away and give it time. Reapproach, talking gently. Slowly reach to stroke its head. If it does not allow a touch, wait awhile and try again. When you can touch the head, gently stroke between the ears and down the back of the head. If the growling starts, remove your hand. When the cat begins to feel secure, it will start to relax and stop growling. This may take anywhere from a few hours to a few days.

Case History Malachi was about eight months old when he came to live with me. He was twice adopted and returned to a shelter with claims of being mean. It took about two weeks of using the above method before we made friends, and within a month he was a purring lap cat with a love of attention.

He is a big blue Persian with a ferocious look, but underneath that exterior he was a scared kitten. He growled to show he was insecure and stressed, not because he was mean. The growl is a defense communication used when a cat is frightened or angry. When he felt secure, growling was replaced by purring.

If Malachi's first home had allowed him to make the first move, he would have adjusted well because Persians are quiet, gentle cats. Since Malachi did not immediately fit the first new owners' expectations of a Persian, it was assumed he was mean and nasty.

Ming of Hope Haven. *James Curtis*

An abused cat cringes from the human hand until it learns to trust again.

James Curtis

Cringing

The physically abused cat will cringe from the human hand. To teach this cat to trust requires a great deal of time and effort. The love and trust of this cat is not readily won and may take months to secure.

Case History   Ming was a small kitten when found on a highway. She suffered from starvation, parasites and visible bruising. The physical problems were rapidly dealt with, but the long road of healing her psychological injuries had only just begun.

By her injuries it was obvious she had been beaten with hands and feet. She would freeze in a cringing position when touched. Her eyes seemed to beg not to be hit again, and her entire body quivered with fright. She never gave any vocal signal indicating a warning or anger.

The method I used with her was to reach out and stroke her for a few minutes while talking softly. Then I would gently pick her up and continue to love her with vocal reassurances. During this process I would try to maintain eye contact, as this seemed to give her a small measure of comfort. It took about six months of many of these short daily sessions before she would willingly come to me. It was another six months before I heard her purr for the first time. By then she was sleeping at the foot of my bed at night and beginning to play with the other cats.

Her change to a happy, loving companion did not come overnight. It took a great effort on my part to earn her trust and loyalty. She had been so deeply traumatized I often wondered if I would ever break through her wall of fear. It required an enormous amount of patience and courage not to give up working with her at times, as progress was slow. Many times I had to defend to others my reasons for keeping her, as she did not present the image of a happy household cat.

Antisocial Behavior

Cats can be forgiven for avoiding some people some of the time, but some cats are fearful and avoid people at all times. Generally, the reason for this is the lack of sustained human contact in the early months of life or the experience of being abandoned.

This cat exhibits general nervousness and withdrawal. It may crouch immobile, with its pupils dilated. It may refuse to eat or groom itself. It may urinate where it sits because it is too stressed to move.

It will take patience and tender loving care to establish a healthy relationship with this cat, and it may take some time before the cat is able to spontaneously show affection. The cat should be worked with in the same manner as the growling and cringing cat.

Bubba.

The Aggressive Cat

It is normal for a cat to exhibit some aggression toward other cats or humans in defense of its home territory or when out in a new environment. Tail-pulling and teasing in a former home may have made the cat aggressive. This cat may tend to nip or bite the hand that feeds it as a result of the abuse it has endured.

Treatment of this behavior should begin immediately after the cat is shown its new home. Begin by discouraging any nips or bites with a firm "no" command, coupled with a gentle flick on the nose. Never feed the cat after an attack of aggression. Feeding will only reinforce its negative behavior. Instead, wait an hour or so until the cat is calm and placid and accepts being petted.

If the cat is exhibiting aggression toward other cats in the household, this behavior can be discouraged by firmly telling the cat "no" and squirting it with water from a plant mister at the same time.

Normal or Neurotic?

It is difficult to decide what is normal or abnormal feline behavior, because this can depend on an owner's expectations. Scratching furniture is normal behavior for the cat, even though that behavior may be unacceptable to an owner. Such behavior must be considered undesirable rather than abnormal or neurotic. A cat can be trained to redirect this undesirable behavior.

Cats learn by repetition of a sequence of stimuli, response and reinforcement. The relationship between a cat and owner is a delicate one and is easily undermined if the owner uses an inappropriate technique to mold the cat's behavior.

Examples of neurotic symptoms are depression, overeating, loss of appetite, attacking the new owner, and self-mutilation. If the rescue is exhibiting neurotic behavior, consult your veterinarian to rule out physical disease. Overeating can also be caused by an infestation of intestinal parasites.

Treatment for a neurosis that has no apparent physical basis may take many different forms, depending on the cat and the behavior. Sometimes the symptoms can be treated without understanding the cause.

The cat that is easily spooked or startled is generally thought to be a neurotic. This is not always the case. Sometimes there may be physical problems that cause the cat to spook at strange or loud noises.

Case History Bubba is an example of this type. His current owner found him as a small, six-week-old kitten in some bushes beside their home. Today he is a happy, secure cat. He interacts well with the other cats that share the house and his humans. However, the least little odd or loud sound startles him and sends him bolting to hide for short periods. The sound of aluminum foil tearing is enough to send him running for cover.

Look at the picture on the opposite page and note the wedge shape of Bubba's head, forming a triangle, and the long tubular body. These are characteristics of the Siamese and probably indicate Siamese ancestry.

Malachi, Sabrina and Shad, three well-adjusted rescues playing together.   *James Curtis*

The Siamese gene can cause an aberrant nerve connection between the brain and eyes. When this happens, cats have poor three-dimensional vision. It is possible that Bubba inherited this gene defect and has a vision problem. If this is so, then it would be natural for him to become startled at something he does not see clearly and may explain his behavior. By understanding his behavior pattern, his owner knows Bubba is not neurotic but acting normal for a cat with a vision problem.

REWARDS OF THE RESCUE

Cats with severe physical trauma are generally left to die along the roadway or in some isolated spot. Occasionally such a cat may be taken to a veterinarian or shelter to be painlessly euthanized. The most common attitude toward the cat with these severe injuries is, is it worth the expense? Yes, it is indeed worth the expense!

We can rekindle a rescued cat's trust only when we can recognize the stress and trauma the cat has endured. When we give this animal our love, effort and patience, we are rewarded with its undying devotion and loyalty.

The rewards of the rescue are long term and lasting. Often the bond that forms with these cats is deeper than the bond with the kitten that spends its life in the same secure household.

14

Showing the Household Cat

COMPETITIVE CAT SHOWS have existed for over a century. The first public cat exhibition can be traced to the 1598 St. Giles Fair, held in Hampshire, England. For many years cats were commonly exhibited at local fairs.

Harrison Weir conceived the idea of selectively breeding and showing cats toward the end of the nineteenth century. He established the first show standard, known as Points of Exhibition and used today in England. On July 13, 1871, he staged the first major show at the Crystal Palace in London. This marked the start of the cat fancy.

In 1895 James H. Hyde organized the first show held in the United States. This show, held at Madison Square Garden, was modeled after those Crystal Palace shows and heralded the birth of the cat fancy in America.

Today there are hundreds of cat shows held every year. In the United States there are several associations with affiliate clubs in every state.

Show rules and procedures vary somewhat among the different cat associations. Basically, cats are selected on a point system or evaluation of the overall quality and closeness to meeting a set, written standard for that breed.

There are several categories for competition. Each show has Kitten, Championship, Alter and Household Pet classes. The classes are divided into longhair and shorthair, and each breed is judged separately. Within the breed divisions are the individual color classes.

The Household Pet class is for those cats not eligible for championship

Friskie, owned by Susan Jones, HHPCC Best Cat of the Year 1983–84.

status. Cats that are random bred or with parentage unknown may be shown in this class. The cat does not have to be registered to be shown, although some associations require the cat to be recorded within a certain time after being shown to be eligible for any points earned toward a Household Pet title. Most cat fancy associations offer a championship title for the household pet.

ENTERING A SHOW

It makes no difference whether you are showing a household pet or a purebred, as the formalities for entering a show are the same. It may be necessary to belong to a local club to enter a show. Shows are generally announced several months in advance in most cat magazines, and they contain the pertinent information on how to enter.

Write the show manager or entry clerk for a schedule and entry form several weeks in advance. Most shows close their entries two to three weeks before the show. The entry form asks for the name, date of birth, color of cat, eye color, long or short hair, sex, sire, dam and breeder. Often, with a household pet, you will not know the date of birth, parentage or breeder, so write "unknown" for those. Make sure all the details pertaining to your cat are correct. This information on the entry form will appear in the show catalog.

The name used on the entry form for your cat is the name that must be used if you register the cat with an association after the show. Unless you have a registered cattery name, you may not use a name with the words "of something." This designation is reserved to show a cattery name.

When my Shalimar was first shown, she was listed in the catalog simply as Shalimar. Since then, I registered "Hope Haven" as a cattery name for the rescues and "Ashkarr" for my silver Persians. She is now listed as Shalimar of Hope Haven. This designates she is from the Hope Haven Cattery. Most do not have a cattery name for household pets. Cattery names are registered by breeders to show a particular cat is their breeding from their cattery. I did this because I show several household pets that are rescues. This is my way of demonstrating that these cats are as special to me as are my silver Persians.

Most shows no longer have a veterinarian at the door to check your cat. You may be asked to sign a declaration that the cat is in good health, or exhibitors may use the honor system. All cats must be vaccinated against the main feline diseases prior to the show and be free of contagious diseases.

SHOW PREPARATIONS

It is important to keep your cat in good condition even if you only show infrequently. This involves providing a good diet and plenty of exercise. Most people who show long-haired cats do not allow them to roam outside because of the risk of badly damaging the coat. Of course, there is considerable sentiment against allowing any cat outdoors.

Shalimar of Hope Haven with her rosettes. *Larry Johnson*

Ming of Hope Haven has been picked for a Household Pet final at an ACFA show. *M. Pyles*

Two months before the show, begin experimenting with bathing the cat. Almost no two experienced exhibitors use the same shampoos or conditioners. The best advice is to find what works most effectively for your cat.

Keep track of how many days after the bath it takes for the coat to return to peak condition. Usually a short-haired black will look its best if bathed three days before and a longhair the day before the show. Some owners of dark-colored cats use a light application of Listerine or bay rum to give a final gloss just before the show. A shorthair can be given a sleek sheen by smoothing the coat with a chamois or silk cloth just before going into the ring.

The ears, eyes and teeth must be absolutely clean. The claws should be trimmed the day before the show. Do not feed a fishy or strong-smelling food the morning of the show, as this causes bad breath. The cat must be immaculately groomed and free of fleas and flea dirt. Cleanliness counts a great deal in the judging of household pets.

Your cat should be conditioned to be handled by strangers before the show. It will be on constant view at the show hall. Take advantage of visitors to your home and have them handle your cat.

SHOW DAY

Most shows require that you check in about an hour before the judging starts. At the hall you are given a catalog and told where you are benched. You need this time to set up your cage and settle in before the big moment arrives.

The cats are kept in a section of cages called the benching area. The show cages are generally 24 inches deep, 26 inches wide and 22 inches high for one cat. If you have entered two cats, the cage is 52 inches wide. There is a wire door in the middle of a double cage that is closed to make the single cage.

You need curtains or toweling to drape the sides and back of the cage. These drapes can be fastened with safety pins or clothespins. Be sure the material you use is washable and does not have glitter or any other substance that can irritate the cat's eyes. Cage drapes can be plain or fancy. Some clubs even award a prize for the best-decorated cage. Line the bottom of the cage with a soft mat or pad for your cat's added comfort.

Take a small cushion or soft bed for the cat, if it has a favorite, and include a couple of toys so it can amuse itself on the bench. Food, dishes, litter and trays may not be provided, so take your own. Most people will take dry or semimoist food. The show flier will give all this information.

Household pets are divided into longhair and shorthair classes. In an all-breed ring, the top ten finals are made after both classes are judged. In a speciality ring, the longhairs are judged and the top five finals awarded. The process is repeated for the short-haired cats. The presentation to the Best Household Pet in Show is given at the end of the day. The same rosettes used for championship classes are used for Household Pet class finals.

The most important thing about showing the household pet is that many are

Cats resting in the benching area between judging rings. *M. Pyles*

ACFA Judge Ron Murphy awards his Household Pet finals. *M. Pyles*

redeemed rescues that would not have had a chance to live much less be in a cat show if someone had not cared enough to give them homes. The mere fact the cat is entered in a show makes both the cat and the owner winners!

Listen for your cat's number. When it is called, take the cat immediately to the ring. There will be a group of small wire cages with numbers on top of them. Place your cat in the cage with the number corresponding to your entry number. Do not remove the cat until the judge or ring clerk indicates the judging is completed. Once your class has been completed, listen for the finals to be announced. If your cat is one of the lucky finals, you must return the cat to the ring.

As the day progresses, you may accumulate ribbons for your cat's wins. These are customarily hung on the outside of the cage. If you are attending a two-day show, leave the ribbons from the first day on the cage. Show rules require that you stay for the duration of the show. If your cat has been judged and is no longer in competition, you still may not leave without permission of the show manager and then only for a good reason. The general public pays an admission fee to come into the show hall to see all the cats, and the management wants the public to see them. At the close of the show, clean the cage of litter trays and paper litter before leaving the hall.

REGISTERING THE HOUSEHOLD CAT

Some cat associations record household pets in a manner similar to what is used with purebreds and have title systems just for the household pet. To receive credit for points earned at these shows, the cat must be recorded. Each association has different rules for recording. Contact the appropriate association immediately after the show. You may also contact them to register your cat prior to a show.

THE HAPPY HOUSEHOLD PET CAT CLUB

The Happy Household Pet Cat Club (HHPCC) is to the household pet what the other associations are to the purebred. This organization was founded in 1968 and pursues a number of priorities. The promotion of the welfare of all cats and public education are high on the list, along with the promotion of spay and neuter programs. Fostering cooperation with the purebred cat fancy and upgrading the status of the household pet are also included in the club's goals.

Over the years a main office has been established. Membership has expanded across the United States and Canada, making the HHPCC an international organization. There is a written set of standards for other associations to adopt on judging. A system of registering cats is maintained which includes an individual registration number for each cat.

The association publishes a newsletter, *The Happenings*, containing show

Judge begins her general examination.

Larry Johnson

reports, news about upcoming shows, informative articles on cat welfare and health, product reviews and legislation of interest to cat owners.

HHPCC annually awards honors to the top ten cats and five kittens in each of the sixteen regions as well as nationally. For a cat to be eligible for these awards, the owner must be a member of the HHPCC. The cats do not have to be registered with HHPCC to be eligible for a regional or national award.

SHOW STANDARD FOR HHPCC

General Description

The ideal household Pet Cat comes in every color you can imagine. Mother Nature has designed the Household Pet according to her own unwritten Standard of physical beauty. She combines body type, eye color, tail length, coat length, color and pattern in ever-varying combinations. She adds personality with a liberal dash, sometimes favoring the sweet, shy little charmer; sometimes the outgoing clown. Occasionally, she gifts a Household Pet with the distinguished demeanor of an international diplomat. By now, we all know that it's a very poor idea to question Mother Nature: Therefore, this Standard does not attempt to define the perfect Household Pet according to its physical appearance or personality. We simply indicate the relative importance of these categories by assigning them a specific number of points. Final decisions as to Beauty and Personality will remain, as always, in the competent hands of our judges.

The category of Condition is the most important part of the Household Pet Standard. We recognize and deplore the serious overpopulation problem in cats, and our Standard has been prepared with this problem in mind. No pet can be bred to meet this Standard. The Household Pet must be properly cared for to meet this Standard. The ideal Household Pet is scrupulously clean, well-fed and altered. He seems to smile with good health and contentment. He occupies his position as Head of the Household with serious pride.

Detailed Description

Beauty—25 points   These points shall be assigned according to the taste of the individual judge. Judges may notice pleasing markings, colors and patterns. Overall grace and balance are often factors to be considered in the determination of beauty.

Personality—15 points   The Household Pet should be alert, friendly and easy to handle.

Allowances should be made for certain Household Pets that behave nervously, due to lack of familiarity with shows.

Condition—60 points

1. Condition of the coat: 25 points. The coat must be absolutely clean and free of any trace of mats or parasites. The cat must be well-groomed. The coat should have a pleasant gloss or sheen.

Bandit, owned by Dorothy Lewis, was the HHPCC Best Cat of the Year in 1974-75.

Chanan

Bandit is shown here after losing her eye to cancer. She still continued to win her share of finals, proving that a cat with imperfections can still be a winner! *Chanan*

Chocolate Eclair, owned by Marie Phetteplace, HHPCC Best Cat of the Year,
1987–88 and 1988–89.

2. Eyes, ears, teeth and breath must be absolutely clean. Eyes and nose must be free of any matter. 15 points.
3. The cat must be at a proper weight in proportion to its size. The cat shall be penalized just as heavily for overweight as for underweight. 10 points.
4. In view of the tragic overpopulation problem in cats, all Household Pets should be altered. 10 points.

Withhold All Awards

All awards shall be withheld from any Household Pet that is obviously dirty or in poor condition. All declawed cats shall be withheld.

Appendix A

Cat Associations

American Cat Association
8101 Katherine
Panorama City, CA 91402
(818) 782-6080

American Cat Fanciers Association, Inc.
P.O. Box 203
Point Lookout, MI 65726
(417) 334-5430

Cat Fanciers' Association, Inc.
1309 Allaire Avenue
Ocean, NJ 07712
(201) 531-2390

Cat Fanciers' Federation, Inc.
9509 Montgomery Road
Cincinnati, OH 45242
(513) 984-1841

Happy Household Pet Cat Club
c/o Mrs. Dorothy Lewis
260 Corral Avenue
Sunnyvale, CA 94086
(408) 732-2574

The International Cat Association
P.O. Box 2684
Harlingen, TX 78551
(512) 428-8046

Appendix B

Household Cats of the Year Honor Roll

<small>AMERICAN CAT ASSOCIATION</small>

Season	Cat	Owner
1983–84	Lady Veronica	Sylvia Jacobs
1984–85	To Jo No's Scotter	Joan Nobel
1985–86	Fluttertoes Twenty-one	Linda Mosher
1986–87	Kitty Cadbury	Karen Harkins
1987–88	Fluttertoes Twenty-one	Linda Mosher
1988–89	Just Fern	Heather Swader

<small>AMERICAN CAT FANCIERS ASSOCIATION</small>

1981–82	Apatchee	Jean Damoce
1982–83	Butterfly	Dr. Herbert Lida Vent
1983–84	Dream Sweet Seymour Fish	Will & Lillian Walter
1984–85	Winston	Allen Donlan and Julia A. Martens
1985–86	Pebbles	Audrey Kochalyk
1986–87	Hawaiian Sunshine	Steve and Lori Vande Wiele
1987–88	Autumn's Kaleidoscope	Frances Lee and Jean Damoce
1988–89	Harley	Judy Ingram

Cat Fanciers' Federation, Inc.

1981–82	Feather O'Rica	Gary and Shelley Ilnicky
1982–83	Feather O'Rica	Gary and Shelley Ilnicky
1983–84	Karate Kat	Toby Lynn Schwartz
1984–85	Feather O'Rica	Gary and Shelley Ilnicky
1985–86	Ilsmadora Lunacy	Barbara R. Fearing
1986–87	Bartholemew	Claire Hollister-Singer
1987–88	Savoir Faire	Arty and Sheri Mitchell
1988–89	Savoir Faire of Arubacats	Arty and Sheri Mitchell

Happy Household Pet Cat Club

1972–73	Lady Charles II	Bob Kaminski
1973–74	Buttercup	Mary Danko
1974–75	Bandit	Dorothy Lewis
1975–76	Lucky	Mary Scullion and Louise Rowley
1976–77	Maegan	Tami Ellis
1977–78	Tinker Mack Toy	David and Carolyn Vane
1978–79	Sweetie Pie	Mary Danko
1979–80	Pedro	Karin Jackson
1980–81	The Cisco Kidd	Ted and Reta Hiatt
1981–82	Harry	Mildred Smith
1982–83	Harry	Mildred Smith
1983–84	Friskie	Susan Jones
1984–85	Tamara's Blaze	Deborah and Carolyn Wisz
1985–86	Tamara's Blaze	Deborah and Carolyn Wisz
1986–87	Woodpile	Cheryl Nakao
1987–88	Chocolate Eclair	Marie Phetteplace
1988–89	Chocolate Eclair	Marie Phetteplace

The International Cat Association

1979–80	Tucker	Wanda Rodriguez
1980–81	Peppermint Patty	Suzanne Servies
1981–82	Tequila Sunset	Bill and Brenda Kinnunen
1982–83	Sammy of Tulane	Chris and Marian Jambor
1983–84	Annbirwave's Caboose	Jared and Ann Hoehn
1984–85	Kitti Kat's Moose	Katherine Marshall
1985–86	Midstar's Caviar	James and Jennie Stewart
1986–87	Lotta La Feet	Suzanne Servies
1987–88	Chocolate Eclair	Marie Phetteplace
1988–89	Chocolate Eclair	Marie Phetteplace

Appendix C

Cat Magazines

Cat Fancy
11760 Sorrento Valley Road
San Diego, CA 92121

Cats Magazine
P.O. Box 4106
Pittsburgh, PA 15202

The Morris Report
303 North Glenoaks Boulevard #600
Burbank, CA 91502

Purrrrr!
The Meaow Company
HCR 227 Rd.
Islesboro, ME 04848

Appendix D

Cat/Animal Welfare Groups

The American Humane Association
Animal Protection Division
9725 East Hampden Avenue
Denver, CO 80231
(303) 695-0811

The Delta Society
P.O. Box 1080
Renton, WA 98057

The Humane Society of the United States
2100 L Street, N.W.
Washington, DC 20037

The Morris Animal Foundation
45 Inverness Drive East
Englewood, CO 80112
(303) 790-2345